I0140790

Living While Liz

ELIZABETH WIGGINS

Published by ELIZABETH WIGGINS, 2025.

While every precaution has been taken in the preparation of this book, the publisher assumes no responsibility for errors or omissions, or for damages resulting from the use of the information contained herein.

LIVING WHILE LIZ

First edition. June 17, 2025.

Copyright © 2025 ELIZABETH WIGGINS.

ISBN: 979-8990789623

Written by ELIZABETH WIGGINS.

Also by ELIZABETH WIGGINS

Living While Liz
Living While Liz

This book is dedicated to all those, in my past and present, who have always stood by me and encouraged me. I especially thank my family who support and keep me humble in each of my pursuits. I thank God every day for those who consider me a part of their village.

I Couldn't Wait to Get Out of There!

Some folk think things must be compartmentalized. Should they be, though? If I am in class, I should be in class.

If I am at the doctor's office, I should be at the doctor's office. Each needs your undivided attention. Never should our ever-moving worlds co-exist. But why shouldn't the adventures of a doctor's office visit meld nicely with the adventures and ups and downs and joys and amusements penned by writers in my creative writing class? Well, I'm a witness that in this world of Zoom, it is quite possible for the two to mesh.

I was sitting in the urgent care department, waiting to be seen. I kept peering at my watch and noting the passing of each minute. It was getting closer and closer to 10:00, the time that my creative writing class would begin. The pain in the pointer finger on my right hand had led me to this place. I had hit it on the refrigerator door at the Giant grocery store where I went to purchase some milk. That hit was the last straw. The pain that shot through my finger made me lean over the grocery store cart for a minute or so and just hold my hand. This was my feeble attempt to cover the pain I was feeling from anyone who might be walking by. I pulled myself together, made a call to get an appointment, and went to the urgent care center.

There I sat, waiting to be called by the doctor while simultaneously waiting for my class to begin. I enjoyed the class because I got to hear so many creative ideas and words penned on paper, which were then verbally shared in class each week. I figured if I had to be in urgent care, I could at least enjoy time listening to my classmates. And yet, I could not wait to get out of that medical facility.

My thoughts of disease, infection, needles, tests, waiting, and waiting ran rampant through my mind until class mercifully began. My classmates were talking about their writing week when I was called back to see the doctor.

1

Their voices faded to a whisper, as he said, "You have an infection in your cuticle. We can take care of that." "Okay," I tentatively replied. 'This after only looking at my finger for a second?' I thought to myself.

"We can go one of two ways. I can give you a soak for your finger that you will use for a few days to see if that will take away the infection and swelling. The other option is to numb your finger and then drain your finger by cutting here."

He was pointing to the left side of my finger halfway down the nail. "To completely numb your finger, I will need to give you three injections here, here, and here" He pointed to three places around the base of my pointer finger.

Before I could say enthusiastically, I'll take option number one and soak my finger; he continued, "If I give you the soak, it may or may not work. Four out of Five times, people come back and still have to have their fingers drained."

Enthusiasm gone, face pulled down in a frown, I off looked into the distance and heard my classmate tell our class about a mistake.

The doctor must have sensed my concern because his voice cut through my classmate's reading. "I'll be right back.

Think about it, and then you can tell me what you decide."

I allowed myself the luxury of forgetting my dilemma for a moment as I listened to my classmates give encouraging feedback and our teacher point out ways to enhance the piece.

Then, the doctor returned and immediately began talking. "Okay, what did you decide?"

I was glad he didn't say what did we decide. That bothers me. "If you choose to drain it now, it will be done and over".

"I don't like needles. But if it will be over, I guess I will have it drained now." My voice sounded small even to me. I was hearing. about a smart business move that began with purchasing some property, and then I got dropped from Zoom.

"I will be right back with the instruments I need."

Was it my imagination, or did he seem pleased to be about to stick my finger?!

You would have thought I lost a lifeline the way I quickly punched keys and maneuvered screens to get back into my Zoom class. "Success!" I pushed the mute button just as the doctor returned to the room.

Another round of classmates and our teacher sharing thoughts on the piece thankfully held most of my attention, taking me somewhat out of my moment. The other half of my attention was tuned into watching the doctor getting things ready.

Then, I listened to a moving story about a war veteran. The telling of that experience was captivating, but I was brought back to my reality because that doctor was bringing a needle toward my recently disinfectant-swabbed finger. I looked away and concentrated on listening to my classmate's voice. I shook ever so slightly as I felt the first insertion and the slight rotation of that needle.

I thought he had said three needles altogether! However, three more times, the doctor would insert and wiggle that needle. Three more times, I would allow the voice of a classmate or our teacher to dull my senses even as three more times, I would shudder. Three more times in three new places before he considered my finger numb enough to drain.

The doctor then picked up the instrument to lance my finger, and I intentionally turned my attention back to what was going on in class. The reading of the war story and the comment time were ending, and another writer was about to begin sharing. While I was concentrating on the class, I did not notice what the doctor was doing. The lancing was so quick that I only heard the doctor say, "It's done."

"It's done?!!" I exclaimed.

"All done. They will bring your paperwork, and you will be able to go"

I hopped off that table and noticed I had once again been kicked out of the Zoom class. I almost forgot I needed to get the paperwork. I wanted to get out of there!

The nurse came back in, wondering why I had not left the room. I think because I was standing and looking like I was ready to jet out of there she didn't think to cover my finger. I was standing in the middle of the floor, holding my finger up and looking at it in disbelief. Something in me registered as I looked back down at my finger, which was still bleeding and unbandaged.

"Oh, I see," said the nurse, noticing things as well. "We still need to wrap up your finger." Then everything made sense, and it fully dawned on me that I couldn't leave like that.

She bandaged my finger, gave me my paperwork, and said I was all done.

I jetted out of there and ran-walked my way back to my car that was parked in the dimly lit garage. I did not tune back into class right away, because reception in the garage was very bad. I turned out of the garage and moved to a parking place in the outdoor parking lot. I quickly punched the buttons again and tuned back into my Zoom class. I waited for the sound to begin to come through my car door speakers and began to listen as another classmate told us about "Snowflakes from Heaven."

Yes indeed! I couldn't wait to get out of that emergency room with all its needles and lances and back into my class. I was back in a comforting place where I could listen and enjoy the rich, well-thought-out arrangement of words my classmates were sharing.

Lost and Found

I had to start school in Headstart because my birthday was in November, after the cut-off for five-year-olds to begin kindergarten. I don't remember much about Headstart, except that I would walk to school with a set of twins and their grandmother. They were my friends, and their grandmother was kind to me. I also remember that Headstart was the first place where I simply refused to eat vegetables. I felt I did not have to eat them at school, like I did at home. The teacher called and told my mother, but I do not remember getting into any trouble over it. I have memories of a dark classroom. It seemed like the lighting was just dreary. Other than that, I don't remember anything – not how my teacher looked, not what I learned, nor what the other children looked like. Nothing. Strange. It was as if I were lost in a maze...

So, I was three months shy of being six years old when I started kindergarten. Kindergarten was half a day. I went to school in the mornings during the first two quarters of the school year. I walked with my older brother and sister to school without ever worrying about getting there and back home. They were responsible for ensuring I made it to school and back safely.

I had to go to school in the afternoon for the second two quarters because my older siblings were in school all day. Otherwise, I would be walking to school alone. So, after I had lunch for the first few days, my Mom walked me to school. She explained that I should pay attention because I would soon have to walk alone.

The day came when it was my turn to go solo. When my Mom walked me to school that afternoon, she said, "Elizabeth, I will be waiting for you at the bottom of the hill."

I went about my school day, knowing I would be walking home alone. I was ready to take this step. I started out towards home, trying to remember the way. I had been so comfortable with my siblings and Mom that I didn't pay close attention to the route. I walked and took turns and thought I should see my Mom, but I didn't. I went down a hill, but I was just unsure. So, I did what I knew how to do when I was not sure and felt helpless – I cried.

I remember a lady seeing me crying. She asked, "What's wrong? Why are you crying?"

I sobbed, "I can't find my way home. My Mom said she would wait for me at the bottom of the hill, but I cannot find the place. I know there is a mailbox, but I don't see it!"

The lady walked with me a little way and pointed to the bottom of the hill. I actually was only around the corner, half a block up the hill. I would have seen my Mom if I had just walked a little further. I saw that mailbox, but better still, I saw her. I took off running to my mother, and I think that was my first memory of hugging her. I just remember how safe that hug made me feel.

That would not be the last time I would experience agony of being lost and the joy at being found.

The Dualism of Falling

I no longer feared getting lost walking that ¾ of a mile to school. Kindergarten was wonderful, bright, cheerful, and full of possibilities. A virtual dream come true for a girl eager to learn new things. I happily put on a pretty rust-colored jumper dress. The only bad part was putting on those ugly bone-colored old people's Oxford shoes (Exactly! What color is bone?). Two pigtails and braided plaits crisscrossed across my forehead for bangs—I felt that I looked nice enough so that my coke-bottle thick-lensed eyeglasses would not be noticed. So, I got my lunch bag, and off I trotted to school.

In my child-like, excited mind, I believed our class was going well until the time came to choose a play station. We could spend time in the kitchen, the building blocks corner, or the reading station. There was also an art section and a truck square.

I headed for the kitchen section. A girl bossily said, "You are not pretty enough to play with me".

Crushed and hurt that someone would say I wasn't pretty and couldn't play in the kitchen, I went away. Even though I could not read, I sat alone at the reading station. In the days that followed, I didn't go near her. My teacher asked if I wanted to play. I just shook my head, said no, and stayed in that corner.

A few weeks later, I was walking and skipping to school, relishing my awareness that I now knew my way to and from school. I was about a block and a half away from home (it was that same corner where I had gotten lost). The tomboy in me took over, and I climbed on a center-block wall to test my balancing skills. That two-foot-tall gray brick wall wasn't secure; it collapsed, and I fell, and a brick hit my toe hard. I didn't want to be late for school. So, off I limped, hopped, and cried uphill and down the other eight blocks to school. By the time I arrived, I was in so much pain that I could only go to the office and cry.

"What's the matter? Why are you crying?"

"My foot hurts," I sobbed.

"Can you walk over here?"

I shook my head and sobbed some more.

"Well, we have to call your parents."

My Mom came and took me to the hospital, where we were told I had a broken toe. Leaving my toes out, they wrapped wet pieces of what I later learned was gauze around my foot and leg. They covered the gauze with a wet substance. My eyes widened in amazement as I saw how that white sticky stuff hardened into a cast that went up to just under my knee. This would be my sock and shoe until my toe healed.

In class the next day, to my pleasant surprise, everyone fussed over my cast and went out of their way to make sure I was comfortable. When our teacher asked us to sit in a circle on the floor for reading, I was given a chair. My classmates even signed my cast!

That day, when the time came to play in our stations, that same bossy little girl invited me to play in the kitchen. Happy and surprised, I joined her in the kitchen.

When we saw each other as adults, I never asked whether she remembered our first kindergarten encounter when she knocked me down. But I think fondly about how falling down and breaking my toe helped me get back up.

Dance Memories

Today is Monday, January 16, 2023. It is Martin Luther King Jr.'s birthday holiday. I just finished watching the Alvin Ailey Dancers on Live with Kelly & Ryan. The dancers performed Wade in the Water from Revelations. Two ladies and a gentleman swayed, danced, and moved like graceful swans. The contractions and releases into turns and deep pliés were impactfully mesmerizing and took me to snapshots of long-ago places.

SNAP

I was 22 years old. I would leave work at the Presbyterian Foundation in Manhattan, New York, and head to Midtown, where the Alvin Ailey School of Dance was located. I would arrive around five or 5:30 and quickly peel off clothes until I was in the leotard and tights required for class. Thinking back, I can't believe that I was in good enough shape to wear that outfit without a coverup. Anyway, we would be doing dance routines. The usual bar exercises – tendues, petit bâtiments, grand bâtiments, demi-pliés and grand pliés. We would balancé, and glissade across the floor. We would chané turn and pirouette and grand jèté across that space – all done seemingly effortlessly.

On some nights, I would look around, and there would be Alvin Ailey himself sitting on some sort of stump or block, watching us as we replicated a dance sequence across the floor. At first, I didn't know who he was, but then I realized it was him, and I felt so honored that he was there watching us at that moment. Can you imagine being watched by a dance icon? The drummer would beat out the tempo. We would execute the sequences to the steady, strong, afro-influenced beating of the drum.

We didn't wear ballet shoes; all was done barefoot in that class. The dance instructor would demonstrate the movement once, and then we would have the opportunity to dance across the floor in twos or threes.

Reaching the other side of the dance studio, we would line up to return, doing the sequence with the other leg leading the way. Yes, you had to be a two-sided dancer to succeed in those classes.

I would hang out in that dance studio from the time I got off from work until about nine at night. When I left the studio, I always felt elated and couldn't wait until it was time to return to class and be back in that mesmerizing atmosphere....

SNAP

I was in my teens when we danced to Star Wars. I took lessons at the Mary Anderson School of Dance. That is where I began to dance and would continue throughout high school. This particular year, we were going to dance to Star Wars theme song.

We had costumes that were designed well to help us look like the characters in the movie. Silver, white, black were the main colors. We had knee pads and arm pads. Each of us had a lighted laser sword. There was an R2D2 and a C3PO, Darth Vadar, Luke Skywalker, his second in command, and Princess Leia. I danced the role of Luke Skywalker's second in command. It was a grand number. The lasers lit and the strobe lights flashed as we did the choreographed fight scenes. Each movement was done with precision. The entire dance ended with bows from everyone – from the dance corps down to the seven of us who had lead roles. It was an exciting time because we did the routine while the movie was fresh on the minds of those who attended the recital.

SNAP

I was in high school. I auditioned and got accepted into the Howard D. Woodson Senior High School's Music Major Program. While there, I auditioned for the play "Happy Birthday Black America, written and directed by a music teacher, Grace Bradford. I played the role of one of the hairdressers. The entire cast could dance, act, and sing.

Rehearsals helped us hone our skills. We all respected one another's talents. It was a great opportunity, and maybe it spoiled us for what we thought performing could be. We pretty much cheered one another on. One thing is for sure, it let me know, "Wow, I need to be humble because everyone here is talented!"

Of course, there was some high-school, teenage drama. But for the most part, we recognized the talent that was present. If I could do a grand battement that almost placed my leg at my forehead, someone else could do one and effortlessly move into a triple pirouette. If one person could hit a high B, someone else could hit a high C. It was just talent central, and we all loved performing.

During the hairdresser scene, there came a point where we danced and sang. I remember trying desperately to remain in character when something hilarious happened. There was a teen who played an old woman to perfection. Her makeup was impeccable, and she was a great comedic actress, even at her young age. It was great fun and an opportunity for me to learn how to dance in character.

The play was performed at Ford's Theater and L'Enfant Plaza Theater. So, that made the experience even more valuable and memorable, I never imagined I would be on those stages!!

SNAP

When I was a youth, our church did not allow dancing. Therefore, it was considered radical for two young Christian girls to dance at one of our annual Christmas Family Night Dinners. The main course of the meal was complete. The congregation was enjoying the dessert that the teenagers had served. As servers, we wore red skirts and white turtlenecks.

While they enjoyed dessert, it was time for us to dance. The two of us had choreographed the dance to "Oh Holy Night". We were excited to showcase our gifts. I was thrilled and nervous at the same time. We made a quick change and put on white skirts. I was thankful my Mom had found a way to get me the costume I needed.

The song began, and those gathered recognized the tune – "Oh Holy Night, the stars are brightly shining. It is the night of our dear

Savior's birth." We glided across the stage, doing points and tendues to the side, pulling tenduing foot into fifth position in the back. We chané turned to the right, and chané turned to the left. We bourrée forward and bourrée back. When we heard the lyrics "Fall on your Knees," we were agile enough to drop to our knees, lay prostrate on the floor, then fluidly raise to our knees and then flow into a standing position while moving our arms from second, to first, to fifth, and just as quickly leaning to the side and lifting our hand to our ear as we heard "Oh hear the angels voices."

Our agility continued as we rose to our feet, ran around in a circle, and began our descent into the end of the number. Overjoyed, we walked in opposite directions around to the rear of the stage, where we met in the middle and stepped together to the front of the stage. We did a step arabesque to the left, a step arabesque to the right, a stepped bow to the right a step and lunged into a bow to the left. And one last grand bow as we glanced and smiled at one another and heard the last lines of the song "Oh Night Divine."

We knew we had done our best, and the congregation clapped and cheered for us. That was a magical night!

SNAP

During the pandemic, we had to come up with creative ways to worship. Each year, our church's Gospel Choir presented a Black History Month Concert. We decided to have a virtual concert in 2021.

One of my contributions was to sing, sign, and dance to "We Shall Overcome." Now, I did not know how to sign. Therefore, I had to learn sign language for the song. I sang acapella. I choreographed the movements that would accompany my singing and signing. The singing, the dance, and the signing had to be recorded separately and then blended together in the final video presentation.

I decided to wear a blue dashiki-style dress and found some African-style earrings to complement the dress. With the decision about the outfit out of the way, I turned to the performance part of this endeavor.

Dancing at 61 is not the same as dancing as a child, teen, or young adult. I had to practice and practice and practice some more. I could see the moves in my mind before I could actually execute them. I mentally remembered how to spot and maintain my balance. However, performing those moves took as much practice as learning to sign. This time singing was the easiest part of preparing for this performance.

Creating a video for Zoom was a three-part process. Three recordings were made – singing, signing, and dancing. After completing the three recordings, they had to be merged so that the viewers would see me singing, signing, and dancing simultaneously.

The congregation remarked that they were amazed that I was able to do all three. They said I did a great job. That made me feel good about the effort it took to complete that process.

When you sign to music, it is not just a mechanical effort. For me, it was art. I felt the song as I was signing the words. Signing gave me the same thrill that dancing and singing gave me. I was interpreting the music through signing and dancing. Feeling the words as I sang them was empowering.

These are only a few snapshots of the memories I have as a dancer. Some many years ago, some in my recent past.

No matter when, how, or why I dance, I can see it and feel it as if it were all only moments ago!

Laces Do Tie!

This morning, I woke up, thanked God, and looked over the side of the bed for my bedroom slippers. I reached and put them beside each other, with the left slipper on the left and the right slipper on the right. I knew they *were right because I looked at their toes and made sure they were* pointing straight ahead. I got dressed for my aquafit class. I put on my red swimsuit and my red swim coverup top. I put on red flair capris and a red and white jacket.

I have decided to wear my red Sketcher aerobics shoes. They tie up.

I smile because I can tie my shoes with a single bow. My shoes are on the right feet, and they are tied up. It may seem strange to recall a memory of this kind, but I smile because I remember when I told my Mom and Dad "I will never be able to tie my shoes!"

Oh, the memories...

* * *

It is 1965. I am six years old and about to start Kindergarten. It was bad enough that I could not do this while still in Headstart. But now, I am finally going to school with my older sister and brother. I still cannot figure this thing out! My older sister and brother can do it. My brother, one year younger than me, can do it. What's up with me? I just kept trying. It was useless!

"Elizabeth, you can do this. Come on, let's try again."

I sat on the floor at my Dad's feet, and he got ready to help me again. I muttered to myself. "No matter what you do, I won't get this."

"First, you must know which shoe to put on which foot. Now, look at your feet. Come on, stand up, and look at your feet. Okay, now let's begin again to go over the steps."

I looked down at my feet. They looked right to me. So, I looked at my dad and hunched my shoulders.

"Stand up and put your feet together."

I did as he asked.

"Now, look at the toes of your shoes." He reached down and used his finger to trace around the tips of my shoes. "Do you see that the toes of your shoes are pointing out?

"No," I said, looking sad and shaking my head.

"Okay, sit down and put your shoes on the other feet."

I hung my shoulders, sat down, and switched my shoes.

"Now, stand back up, and let's look again."

I stood up and looked down at my feet. At first, I didn't see the difference.

"Look at the toes of your shoes again. See, how they now point straight ahead?"

I wasn't sure, so I looked at them, twisting my head from side to side.

Sensing my hesitation, my Dad said, "Wait a minute."

He got up, went to his side of the bed, and pulled out a pair of his shoes.

I noticed how his shoes were neatly aligned under the bed. The colors matched, but tennis shoes and dress shoes were separate. He did not have many pairs of shoes, but they were always placed neatly under the bed. My Dad liked things to be neat and clean and didn't mind doing the work to keep things that way. My Mom loved things to be neat and clean, but she was pretty happy when someone else did it for her.

Anyway, Dad returned to where I was sitting in front of his chair and put the shoes on the floor with the left where the right should go and the right where the left should go. "See, look at the toes of the shoes. They are pointed out and away from each other. Now, watch as I switch them."

He switched the shoes, and the light bulb went off in my head, and I smiled broadly.

"I see!! I see!!" Wow, that's one thing I can do now. At least I won't go to school with my shoes on the wrong feet! My smile grew wider with the thought.

"Now, let's look at tying your shoelaces."

His gentle tone did not keep me from slumping my shoulders and losing my smile. I could get the first part where you loop the strings over one another and through and then pull tight. Initially, even that was a little hard to grasp, but I got it.

"That's right," my father smiled. "With one string, now, make a bow like this." His voice was meant to be encouraging.

I made the bow with one string, and then my confidence sank. "Here comes the part I can't get," I said to myself.

Sitting there, sucking my tongue as I do when I am concentrating hard on something, I tried to follow the next step that my Dad was demonstrating. "See, wrap the other part of the lace around that bow in your hand."

I looked and followed closely. I am doing my version of wrapping that lace around that bow.

"Now, you should have two bows." He looked over and nodded because he thought I had two bows. So, pull that bow through that hole and pull both bows tight.

"I'm doing it. I'm doing it. No. I am not doing it at all."

Dad's shoe is tied, and the bow looks nice. I'm looking at what I did, and I have two strings with no bow; just two sides of a string flopping.

Lowering my head, I said, "I just can never see that hole."

He gently and patiently said, "Pull the lace through."

I could not get it to make another bow. "I'm never going to get this!" I was not crying, but I sure wanted to.

"I have an idea." My Dad was still thinking I could do this. So, I had to get ready to try something new.

"Now, watch this. You have the first part. This time, I want you to make a bow like we did before. That's right. Now, take the other side of the lace and make another bow. See, like this."

I am doing what my Dad is doing. I have two bows!

"Put one bow across the other one just like this."

"Lay the bow across the other bow." I am telling myself.

"Now, see my finger sticking through that hole?"

"Yes, I see it."

"Your finger is just like it, too. See it?"

"Yes!!"

"Now put that other bow right through that hole and pull both bows tight."

"Like that?" I asked, starting to get excited.

"Just like that. See, your shoe is tied. Try it on the other shoe."

I did it again. My other shoe was tied, too. I can go to kindergarten with my shoes tied!

I never thought I would be able to tie my shoes like the other kids. You know doing it that one bow way. But at almost six, I did not care.

* * *

I not sure when I finally figured it out and could tie my shoes without making the double bows first. It took a while, but eventually, I got it.

Just like passing the road test to get my driver's license. The same with suffering through one advanced math class after another until, while preparing for the teacher's Praxis Exam, I caught onto the principles behind advanced math.

Yep, it takes me a while to catch on to things that others catch on with the snap of a finger. But when I get it, I have it for life!

My shoe just came loose again, and I smile as I reach over and tie it up! My Dad told me I would learn!

And Then I Knew

These are excerpts from a book in the making combined with a piece that I wrote for my creative writing class.

* * *

1996 – Decided to Stop Hoping – I Did Not Know

Anyway, I don't know what to do anymore. I have to divorce him. The papers are ready. I will let a couple of people look them over, and then I'll file them. He said he wouldn't give me any trouble. But then he changed his mind and said he wouldn't sign. One way or another, I will be free.

CAN YOU BELIEVE I STILL LOVED HIM AND ONLY WISHED HE WOULD CHANGE HIS MIND AND REALLY TRULY WANT TO BE MARRIED TO AND NOT HURT ME? I just wanted that handsome hazel-eyed 6'1" man who made me feel beautiful back. And, since that was not going to happen, I had to let go. So, I prayed and asked God, "Why can't I fix my marriage?" And that night, until I could fall asleep, I cried.

* * *

July 2008 – Decided to Perhaps Hope – Who Knows

Skip,

I left you a message on your phone.

However, I believe Langford said you don't check your messages. So, I'm sending you this short note. You had a nice conversation with Lauren while you visited the other day. Both Lauren and Lynne seemed to be pleased that you visited. I told them that if they let you know they enjoyed your company, instead of just telling me, you would come by more often. So, thank you for going by and visiting with them.

Now, Mr. Wiggins, as for the conversation you had with Lauren about you and me, I was surprised and pleased at the same time. Could there be a possibility or probability that you would still like for us to get back together? It's been 12 years. Why haven't you said anything? Lauren said you have thought about it and that some family friends said something to you also. Now, add those three to the two who cornered me one day after worship service and said that we would be getting back together the last time you were there. Then there is the other church member who tells me my husband has a great Escalade, and we seem to be doing fine. Not to mention the couple who sit near Mom in church and told me our grandchildren look just like my husband.

And then there is the ex who got his ring back and left me an unsolicited opinion saying he had a premonition that you and I had remarried. If living folks are not enough, there are the movies that keep coming on TV lately about couples that drift apart and come back together. So, quite a bit in the air seems to hint or imply that something is up. If this is what you want, we should talk about it. It's already clear that we can greatly assist one another financially.

You just told me you are working at night to make more. If we were together, we could be quite comfortable with what we earn together. We would both have health, dental, and vision insurance. We would be taking care of one mortgage and one set of utilities. We would be able to combine our insurance costs and get a reasonable discount on the number of cars and the house. We would be able to file joint tax returns this year and enjoy the benefit of being able to claim the kids and grandkids because they are on my insurance right now. So, we should be okay financially. Which is definitely an improvement over where we were when we first were married.

In terms of having to deal with the proverbial baggage, our baggage is pretty much the same. Our main baggage is our children, and I don't have to worry about you not wanting to hear about my kids and vice versa. A huge struggle with multi-family couples is the issue of the other family that always comes up. We would not have that issue because my children are your children.

So, what about the compatibility part? I think we've been getting along pretty well lately, but that could be because we mainly discuss the kids. But I wouldn't mind working to become even more compatible. Our son's graduation dinner, breakfast, and other times we have spent together lately have been quite enjoyable.

I especially enjoy the time with family when I don't have to worry about the kids asking me something about you or your family and having to worry about whether someone else is going to have a problem if I say something positive about you. That day my mother called, and I had to leave it made me sad because we were watching a movie together. What about romantically? Well, you would have to tell me. It's easy for me to be attracted to someone I haven't been with for a while because the excitement of something new yet familiar is very intriguing and alluring. So, turn on your romantic charm, and let's see what happens.

Anyway, is that what all the looks have been getting are about?

Yes, I am aware that you watch me and then look away if I catch you doing it. I was beginning to wonder if I had done something to annoy you. So, do you believe we have matured enough to really give this another try? If so, I say let's be bold enough to see where it takes us. At least this time, you already know my name and number.

* * *

November 10, 2022 – Hope Springs Eternal

Well, your dad has celebrated another birthday.

Thinking about this man, I call my husband, still makes me smile. I don't think we share enough about who and why we are. So, I thought I would quickly pen the way I came to know he was the one.

Well, of course, there is that initial feeling of "Hey, this just might work."

I saw him in that People's Drug Store (now CVS) and felt that I looked pretty decent, so I just kept walking past him, acting like I was searching for something, and said to myself, "I think he thinks that I'm pretty decent.

I wore short burgundy/purple shorts to show off my legs – my best asset. Anyway, I caught his eye. Of course, he thought he caught mine first. So, I knew this handsome guy could be the one. (By the way, to young ladies who may read this, the outfit was not necessarily and probably not exactly the right thing to wear to attract a good man.)

Physically attractive, yes. But it wasn't until many years later, when we had decided to try again, that I knew he would be the one. It was the day I really knew he had my back, just as I had his.

They had done something else to me up at that church, and, being pretty upset, I had shared the details with him. Even though I was still upset, we went to church the following Sunday. During a hymn, the situation got the better of me, and I began to silently sob. Not uttering a word, I felt his steadying arm holding me close until the song ended, the tears ebbed, and I could listen to the remainder of the service. At that moment, I knew. Somehow, your father would be vested in making sure we were okay.

Have we had a past filled with ups and downs? Sure! Will we need encouraging support and loving reminders? Yes.

But in that moment, such a small gesture inspired such great hope! I'll always keep hope alive.

And then I knew.

inheritance

This is a different approach to viewing an inheritance. Being a minister, my mind immediately went to scripture about the meek inheriting the earth (Matthew 5:5). Hmm, well, I don't think I would characterize myself as meek. Neither will I be considering the inheritance of the earth in this piece. Nevertheless, there are some worthwhile treasures I have inherited while living as Liz. Take a read and I sure hope you find a novel way consider your inheritance(s) as well.

* * *

Inheritances are passed down through the ages, and we society teaches us to cherish those items. An heirloom, some jewelry, property, clothes, and land – things generally passed between families. The list just goes on and on.

I guess when you get to be my age, it's not surprising that a family member has passed and left an inheritance. Another thing, about being my age is that you no longer seem to care about the material things you may or may not inherit in quite the same way. You may relate to this feeling. If a house is left, that's wonderful, but you may have a house. If a car is left, that's cool, but you have cars. If there is jewelry and anything that can trigger the five senses, you have those things. I thank God for those memories and blessings.

So, how would I capture the notion of an inheritance? What is it really?

I thought about this for days. Until I finally pushed past these opening pensive thoughts and penned a letter to my parents. Part 1 is below.

* * *

A child talks to her parents

Dear Mom and Dad,

Dad, you died too soon. Remember? That was when the world was just beginning to talk about Alzheimer's. You were 65 and me, I was pregnant with your grandson.

Mom, I had so many cherished years with you, because you blessed our souls until you were just three months shy of being 89 years old, 30 years after Dad passed.

And though we all cared for you, I was so grateful that you lived the last few months of your life with me, and I was right there as you took that last deep sigh and passed on to eternal life.

Mom, I know I inherited your ability to care for elders. You tirelessly took care of Dad during his illness. Right, Dad? For more than two years, she cared for you in that small brick house we began calling home when I was about two or three, maybe? As you forgot things or became grumpy, Mom loved and cared for you. And when you were really disagreeable, she would call over your male friends to help bathe and dress you. I never heard her say "I love you" but her actions told it all!

Oh, that's something else I inherited, from you both the understanding of how to treasure lifelong friendships. When the chips are down, those friends will come to your rescue.

Dad, you passed on to me the desire to care for my spouse because you cared for mother as she gave birth to six children. You also cared for her each time she became sick with pneumonia. Each time you were there.

One thing I decided not to inherit was your willingness to pick up her clothes and neatly hang them in the closet: while only shaking your head in silent disapproval.

We may not have had a lot of money, and it was not always safe for a Black family to travel through America, but we still managed to visit so many of the states here in America, right? We'd get in the car and drive to Oklahoma and Texas, Ohio and Pennsylvania, New York, North and South Carolina, Florida, and so many other places.

Some might think it odd, but it was our norm for the two of you to be willing to take your six children and then add a neighbor's son and one of our cousins to come on our summer vacation to Disney World.

Dad, how about all the times you would take us on those long walks to get exercise or when you put all of us in our station wagon and took us to Atlantic City so we could ride the waves in the Atlantic Ocean? Because of you, I understand that when you don't have much money, you can jump in the car and head to the water and ride those larger-than-life waves!

Mom, you decided the family that prayed and played together remained together. So, before there was a thing called Family Reunions, your side of the family would get together every holiday to share a meal and play and enjoy one another's company. Family is what it was all about for you and family is what it is for me now...

Mom and Dad, I inherited your determination to stand up for what is right and to protect my family.

Dad, remember how you went up to my 6th-grade elementary school teacher and told her I was right for refusing to stay after school? She said I had to stay behind because I once again did not want to take my books home. Why should I when I had done my homework in class while they were working on another subject. I told her I could not stay after because I had to get my little brother from his Kindergarten class and walk him home from school. (Remember, Mom, you both told me he could not walk home alone.)

When the bell rang, at first, I sat there huffing and puffing because I **was not** taking those books home. Then my little brother poked his head in the door, saw me, and came towards me.

That teacher asked, "What do you need?

"I have to wait for my sister to walk me home."

"Well, she can't leave now. You go along home."

That's when the big sister spun into action. "Oh no. He cannot walk home alone!"

"Then he will have to wait outside until you decide to take your books."

"No," I said. "Come on, let's go". Off I walked with his hand in mine (okay, I went without those books).

"Get back here, Elizabeth!" I heard her voice as I continued to out of that classroom...

Boy, I thought I would be in big trouble for walking out of that class. Of course, Dad, you and Mom received that call and had to come to school for a parent/teacher conference.

It was your turn, Dad. (Yeah, I remember how the six of us kept you both busy going back and forth to school.) Since I remembered your warning not to let you find out from someone else first, I gave you both my version of what happened the night before.

Dad, when you arrived at my class our gym teacher was talking with my teacher. When he left, it was time for the two of us to sit down with her.

My teacher jumped right to the point, "Elizabeth left class yesterday when I told her she had to stay after until she decided to take her schoolbooks home to do her homework. She just walked out."

I thought, "Oh boy, this is not going to go well." But seconds later, Dad, you came to my rescue!!

"Did she tell you she had completed her homework?"

"Yes, she did."

"Did her brother come to the class?"

"Yes, he did."

"Did she explain that her brother could not walk home alone? Did you tell her brother to go wait outside?"

"Yes, he could not wait in the classroom."

"Then, she could not stay after school, and she was right to take her brother and come home. If she completed her work in class, why did she still need to take her books home; unless you were giving her additional work to do?

Well, Dad, that was one of the times I realized that you would stand up for me and protect me if I was doing the right thing. Inheriting that desire to protect and stand up for right still burns deep in my soul.

Mom, you were right there ready to defend me also. I guess I really needed you both in the sixth grade. Remember, I was supposed to play in the orchestra concert?

First of all, thank you for coming through again by getting my black skirt, white blouse, and black shoes (Man, I was glad I no longer needed to wear those corrective bone-colored shoes!!) Those of us in the orchestra also wore a red piece of ribbon tied around our collars. I was so happy as I came in with my violin and was ready to get in line with the others. That is until the Assistant Principal came up and told me I could not play that night.

Remember how I came crying and said, "I cannot play?

You asked me why and still sobbing, I said, "I don't know."

Off you went to speak to that Assistant Principal, "Why can't my daughter play?"

"Because she went on a class trip without permission."

"What trip did she go on without permission?"

"The class trip" was the Assistant Principal's hurried response. "Children cannot go on trips without parental consent."

You responded, "That was an overnight trip. How do you suppose my daughter would be able to be away from home overnight without my permission? She had my permission. So, there is no reason why she cannot play tonight."

I am still smiling at how I got to play in that concert...

And yes, I do realize that you also left me the knowledge that parents are not only our supporting champions but they also are our disciplinarians.

How about the time the six of us came downstairs early on Christmas morning and found we all had new bikes? Six new bikes, a bike to match our age our and size, and our ability. There were three blue bikes for me and my two sisters and three red bikes for my three brothers. There were other toys, and the boys got a nice race car track.

Remember how your son... (yes, he's my wonderful older brother when he's not getting me in trouble) ...rode his bike around our small, smartly decorated living/dining room area. The five of us knew it was trouble when he lost his balance, and fell on that new race car track?

At the sound of the crash, you both came downstairs frustrated and sent us all back to bed. Christmas morning, and we were sent back to bed!!

Then there was the time when you both got fed up with me jumping over our backyard fence and running off through the neighborhood to play with friends. This went against your rule you repeated over and over again for us to stay in the backyard. Remember Mom; you would watch me hop that fence and take off. Well, this time enough was enough, and when I got back you asked, "Where have you been?"

"To play with my friends."

So, you grabbed my skinny arm and took me off, and I got that talking-to-swatting lesson: "Didn't I tell you...." Swat, swat on the backside... "Not to go jumping over that fence..." Swat, swat. "And running off God knows where."

By now, I'm wailing like you are killing me even though you really are not swatting my backside that hard. So, you stop swatting and continue your verbal lesson, "And having us worrying about where you are. You are not going to do it again now, are you?"

"No", I shrieked like the world was ending.

At some point after I became an adult, you both told me you hated having to swat my bottom because I made it seem like you were killing me. Yeah, probably because I knew that would get you to stop.

You taught me that being a parent would mean I would have to have compassion when disciplining was necessary. I, too, would experience many days when I would still feel that pull of sadness at the need to discipline my children.

Mom and Dad, most importantly, you taught me how people who loved one another should behave. I knew what to look for and insist upon in a husband. I knew that if I loved my children and raised them well (like the two of you did), they would flock to my side in times of joy, sorrow, and need.

Dad, I can remember that when I was dating my one and only boyfriend, you would come whenever I called. You would remind him that I was never alone, and you would always be there for me. You passed down your caring nature by helping my hubby out during our early years of marriage. I recall how he could come to you to borrow your car to get to work when his parents' car was not available.

Mom, remember how you would look up, and my hubby would still come and sit beside you in church even after we had been divorced?

I'm chuckling as I remember how surprised some folks were when we announced we were getting remarried, because they never knew we were divorced.

I inherited the understanding that family time is vital. So many times we sat around our one TV and watched shows like Andy Griffin, I Love Lucy, the Flintstones, Good Times, the Jeffersons, the Cosby's. The way we cleaned house to the soulful sounds of R&B, the twangy lilt of country music, spirit-filled melodies of gospel music, the soothing sounds of jazz, and so many other music genres.

Mom, can you hear yourself telling me 'Elizabeth, you cannot go off in a huff because you are losing the game. You have to be as nice when you lose as when you win." Dad, you would add with that wicked laugh of yours, "And, if you can't be happy, then don't let the others know."

How about those rides when the eight of us would go to that frozen custard place for simple but treasured treats?

Remember that drugstore across the street from the church you were a member of? You know, that store that later moved way down the street? At least it seemed way down the street when we would scoot off to it with a quarter in our hand to get some goodies while us kids waited for the end of the service or some meeting at church to end.

Mom, most of the time when you would go out of town, we went with you. But we did miss you that one time when you went to the usher's convention on the west coast and then on to Hawaii for another week. We did have fun with Dad while you were gone.

Dad, after you retired, you would make us Cream of Wheat more often. Somehow, you could make lump-free mashed potatoes (I later discovered that I, too had that skill). As you grew older, it became harder for you to make mash potatoes and cream of wheat lump-free. But I did not mind. I ate around those lumps because I was eating with you, and we were looking out the Kitchen window chatting about the goings on outside.

Mom, I do a pretty good job of making sweet potatoes because I learned the recipe from you. The same is true about making cornbread dressing.

Mom, singing "Oh Promise Me" and "Because" at my wedding made your day, didn't it?

By the way, Mom and Dad, it was okay that you could not afford for me to be a Debutante because you made me feel like one every day.

The courage it took for you to allow me to go first to Ohio to attend Oberlin and then to New York to pursue dancing. Thank you for your willingness to welcome me back home each time I left as if I were the prodigal child. To love me so hard with so few material things. To fight for me so fiercely. To make me feel strong, even when I wasn't sure I had strength. To patch me up when I burned my stomach while making baby formula for my little brother. To take me to the doctor when that hardball whacked me in the eye. To replace my eyeglasses each time they broke. To believe me and make it all right when I was raped. To make me feel beautiful no matter what...

Oh, can you see how I still encourage your children to hold onto the house so our disabled sister will always have a place to live? I inherited this desire for my children always to have a place to live should they need it.

Mom, you looked after made sure that when your third daughter had an aneurism and stroke would have a place live until she died. That inspired me to have a place for my beautiful granddaughter, who is so capable but still requires assistance in order to be successful. I inherited the determination that family should always have a home.

Dad, I walked with you to church when our car would not work. A long walk to that first church. But not so long to the church where you would be laid to rest. Prayer meetings, Bible study, and watching the two of you as church leaders and deacons.

Remember how the eight of us sang together in the Gospel Choir. Mom, you played the piano on occasions when we sang as a family group.

Mom, we debated so many religious topics throughout the years. I remember how you thought I had become an atheist because I asked you so many challenging questions about different faith traditions.

Mom, one of the last questions you whispered to me was, "I can go and be with Jesus, no?"

I replied, "Yes, you sure can. I love you, Mom." From your last words, I inherited the wisdom to know that if I cling to Jesus, I will be all right. I inherited a faith that tells my heart Jesus is real. I knew for sure that heaven was in your sights and that one day, heaven would be my home too.

These are just a few of the things you left me to cherish. Pearls that I now share with my children and grandchildren. Can you feel how my heart is still warmed? Can you see the smile on my lips and the moisture on my cheeks? I love you both very much. Mom and Dad, you are the true embodiment of my inheritance.

Mom and Dad, who knows, perhaps one day when my kids read this, they will realize the life we have shared, the inheritance you left me, is being passed on to them.

Well, we will have to chat later because I'm a little spent now. Oh, but what an inheritance!!

Rest well, I love you.

Courage and Three Silver Linings

The First Silver Lining

It was January 21, 1987.

I had moved from monthly doctor's visits to bi-weekly doctor's visits. But for the past four weeks, I had doctor's appointments every week.

"Things are coming along well," my doctor said. "However, you are not ready yet to give birth."

My face looking incredulous, I said, "Oh no, she was due today."

"You'll have to be patient for a while longer."

Almost ten months ago, I began this journey of becoming a mother. I knew that some discomfort would be involved. The thought of pain made me a little nervous. Nevertheless, the end result would be worth it. So, feeling both a little disappointed and relieved at the delay, I left the doctor's office and headed home to wait longer for the main event.

Now, I don't know about your mom, but my Mother was well-versed in the homespun methods for encouraging the birthing process. So, she said something like, "Elizabeth, we will just have to see if we can help this process along."

I began her methods by taking long walks. That did nothing.

"Do a little housework. Scrub a floor, but do it on your hands and knees."

"Okay, that's a little odd. But I am ready to try anything to give birth," I said.

Even though I was still nervous about the process, I looked around our mostly carpeted apartment for a way to try this technique. The kitchen floor was free from carpet. I had already scrubbed it a couple of days ago, but I bent down to begin the task anyway.

Of course, I totally forgot that I may not be able to get up off the floor once I finished. But I moved through the process, thinking that surely this would work. I completed the task and put all my weight on a chair to begin pulling myself up off that floor. I had to brace myself on the kitchen table, grunt and groan, and then finally complete the rise to my feet.

Yes, I was back on my feet after scrubbing that floor. Nevertheless, nope. I had a twice-cleaned floor, but my baby was still not ready to be born. There were no cramps. There was no tightening of my abdomen. My unborn child had begun to feel heavy in my belly. But still there no signs of labor.

Somehow, we got tickets to the Bullets' basketball game. They are the Wizards now, but back then, they were still the Bullets. My husband and I were young and didn't have a lot of extra money. It would be a long time before we could afford lower-level seats at a game. So, we were in the nosebleed section.

As I looked up the steps that would take us to our seats, I said to myself, "Surely, this will get labor started."

I climbed the steps, holding onto my husband's back and the rails. Slowly, we climbed. I heard someone say, "Is she going to have that baby here?"

I smiled, thinking of all the ways I had already tried to convince my first child to be born. I am sure I looked quite ridiculous waddling up those stairs with my belly sticking way out.

Every time I stood and cheered, folks probably breathed heavily in and out. But I was determined to enjoy that game and hopefully leave, ready to go directly to the hospital and give birth.

Nope, no such luck. The game ended, and we returned home.

I was still nervous about the process, but I was so ready to be a little lighter around the stomach area. Those were my last thoughts before I went to sleep.

Well, then sometime around February 1st or second, it started. Now, two weeks had passed since the baby was supposed to be born.

I felt those first pains in my abdomen. It caught me off guard, and I screamed. "Oh, that hurts!! I think it's time to go."

My husband and I got things together and made our way to the hospital. I forgot or didn't know about waiting and timing. I felt that pain and said something needed to be done about it. I have a short pain threshold. I didn't even like getting my finger pricked to determine my blood type. That little prick. I laugh out loud, thinking how crazy that comparison was. With my reaction, you would have thought someone pierced my heart."

Anyway, this pain was crazy. "Can I do this?" I asked myself. "I don't know," I responded.

"*Courage*," I told myself. This child will be born soon. And then I just chuckled at my self-imposed dramatics.

When traffic was light, the ride was about 20 minutes from where we lived. Another contraction gripped me as we were on the way. I just moaned. Okay, it was more like a loud groan. My husband didn't know what to do. To his credit, at least he wished he could do something.

We arrived at the hospital. Off we went to the emergency room, where my gynecologist was on staff. My husband had my little overnight bag, wore a Polaroid camera around his neck, and carried cigars in his breast pocket.

The emergency room attendants took one look at my stomach and the look on my face and told my husband to take me to the maternity ward floor.

He pushed me in my wheelchair, and we went towards the elevator. I'm put in a bed when we get to the maternity ward. In what seemed like forever, someone came in and checked me to see if the baby was ready to be born. "Sorry, Mrs. Wiggins, it's not time yet."

"Huh?" I said as my frown deepened.

"No, you will have to go back home. You are not dilated at all."

"What about the pain?" I asked as I looked towards my husband, who was nodding.

"False labor. Come back when the contractions are about 10 or 15 minutes apart or your water breaks."

So, off we went. At least they let me ride back down in the wheelchair. I guess that's something. Luckily, I didn't have another fake contraction on the way home. Fake contraction. It sure felt real.

This scenario would play out a second time. I had the pains. When you are in any form of labor (fake or real), it hurts. I mean, it really hurts. So, we marched off again. Little overnight bag, full of courage, knowing that it was time; this time.

Only to be turned away again.

By this time, the pain was getting worse. I screamed at night. My poor husband grabbed a pillow and covered his face. I seldom smiled because the pain was too crazy.

I was over at my Mom's house. I was so uncomfortable that my Mom said, "We are going back to the hospital."

Breathlessly between contractions, I groaned, "They said don't come back until it's time."

"We're going back to the hospital!"

Off we went. My husband would come later. Up I went to the maternity floor. I knew the routine by now. Get undressed. Put on that ridiculous gown that covers nothing because my stomach is so big now. Climb up on that table that seemed to be 12 feet off the floor. Lay back and moan, groan, and wait. Then, the check and probing only made me more uncomfortable because there didn't seem to be room for the baby and the probing. Then, the determination. "Mom, she's not dilatating. That baby is not ready. She'll have to go back home and wait."

And this is when super moms like mine take over. In that protective way, asserting her will, my mom announced, "This baby was due two weeks ago. You sent her home twice already. My daughter is in pain. She's not leaving until this baby is born!"

So, I stayed at the hospital. The pains got worse, but still, they said I wasn't ready. My husband hadn't arrived. The process seemed to be totally distressing to him.

My Mom said, "This is his baby too. So, it's time for him to come. She went to call him and tell him he needed to get to the hospital. My oldest sister was at the hospital and could stay with me until he arrived.

They still hadn't given me any medicine because I wasn't ready!

At some point, I remember squeezing my sister's hand so hard I heard her say, "You have to let go of my hand." She didn't leave me, though.

The doctor came in and checked me again. He said, "She's not dilating. So, we are going to have to induce labor. Elizabeth, we are going to help this baby along. We will give you something to help encourage her to be born. Once we do, things will begin to happen quickly."

"This really hurts. Will I be given any medicine for the pain?"

"Not yet. Once we induce labor, we will give you something." The doctor said. That was not the response I wanted. So, I didn't feel encouraged!

Another pain ripped through my body, and I thought, "This is never going to end!"

Someone came in – by now, I really did not know who was who. I was just concentrating on getting ready for the next pain. How did I know when they were coming? Because they set the monitor so I could look at it. After so many visits to this place, I recognized when it was time by that line that started getting wiggly and going up. "Oh no, it's about to start again!!" I shrieked.

"Stop looking at that monitor," my sister said.

They did something, and all of a sudden, the pain intensified. I thought I had felt the worst pain. But oh no. It actually got worse. I heard myself say over and over, "This really hurts. Are they going to give me any medicine?"

"They said they would," my sister tried to soothe me with her words.

"Elizabeth, you are dilating, and we are going to give you an epidural. Now, we have to give it to you during a contraction, and you will have to be very still. The needle goes into your spine."

"They are going to give me a needle during a contraction, and I have to be still."

I continue counseling myself, "Liz, you have two choices – this pain or be still while you are in pain and get this needle. Pain. Needle and pain to ease the pain. What a choice!"

They readied everything and then waited. We all were watching that monitor, and sure enough, the line started its dance. I braced myself as I heard a voice. "Okay. It's time. Stay still, and we will get this done."

With all the reserve I could muster, I steeled myself against moving as the pain of labor ripped through my abdomen, and the pinch of that needle seemed to rip into my spine.

And then, all of a sudden, that pain subsided.

A while later, they came in, checked my progress again, and said, "Okay, let's get you to the delivery room. This baby is ready to be born."

By that point, I was drowsy, but I remembered being rolled to another colder room. But that was okay because that pain was not as bad. I cannot really remember when my husband joined us. But somewhere in the fog of labor, I remember my Mom saying, "Okay. You can take over. I'm going home and get some rest. Let me know when your baby is born."

I am covered with a white sheet, and my legs are bent, and my feet are put in the stirrups. I am feeling no pain. The doctor and nurses begin their routine, and soon, they are saying the baby is coming. I feel no pain. They gave me instructions. "Elizabeth, on the next contraction, we will need you to push."

Well, now I can't see the monitor, and I am feeling nothing from below. So, I am not sure what is going on. But all is well because they let me know when to act. "Elizabeth, push."

I felt nothing. So, I do my best rendition of pushing, but because I am not sure I am moving at all, I turn to my husband and ask, "Am I pushing?"

"Yes, you are pushing." He responded.

"She still doesn't seem to want to be born yet." I heard someone say.

Then, I think it was the doctor who said, "We are going to have to help her."

Now, I felt myself lose some of my courage as I wondered what was happening. I saw them pass something that looked like a large spatula.

"We are going to help the baby be born by gently pulling her out." They used that thing and pulled her out as they told me again to push. I think I felt her come out.

"She is here."

While they cleaned her up, they began the process of cutting the umbilical cord. "Mr. Wiggins, would you like to cut the cord?" They asked.

"Okay." He quietly responded.

He cut the cord, and the doctor pushed on my stomach to help me pass the afterbirth.

A few minutes later, they handed me my beautiful newborn baby girl. Today is Tuesday, February 4, 1987, and once again, all is right with the world.

Courage and the first silver lining. Who could ask for more?

On that day, little did I know that I would need courage two more times as I went through this process with my second and third children – more to come as I tell of waiting at home till the last moment for my 9.8-pound second daughter to be born and my 6-pound son who was born naturally sans meds.

* * *

SILVER LINING TWO

I knew, but I did it anyway. It could be more – I don't know, foolhardiness. Whatever the motivation, the reward was and continues to be priceless.

I had just made it through the Christmas holidays. It was 1989, exactly 23 months after the birth of my first child. I had survived childbirth and was reveling in being the new mother of a very well-behaved daughter. As long as she wasn't hungry, she was no problem at all.

So, here I was. Once again, I found myself on the brink of giving birth. From the time I conceived, I began to wonder what made me want to do this again. Having another child in the family was not my concern. I rather liked the idea of a second child. It was going through the birth process again. As best as I could, I pushed these thoughts to the back of my mind. Nevertheless, every now and again, I would think about the first time and get a sinking feeling in the pit of my stomach. Actually, by about the sixth month, it was amazing that I could still get a sinking feeling of nerves in my stomach because my belly was pretty full of my unborn child.

Just a side note here: after my first child, my stomach just disappeared. My breasts went back down to their small size. You would not have known I had given birth. So, the fear of a bad figure was not a concern either.

This time, my belly was just growing and growing, and it actually did not bother me that I was growing and that, once again, my body was stretching out of shape. I knew this was the natural way of things. So, the way I looked, waddling around everywhere, did not give me pause or make me feel horrible. I was extremely happy about this part of being pregnant.

So, what was it? It was the process of giving birth itself.

If I could be Jeannie, that TV character that lived in a bottle and could do magic, I would twitch my nose and have my baby in my arms. Yes, indeed, I would be a happy camper. It is funny that I decided just to test the theory and give an attempt at nose twitching. Laughingly, I reminded myself, "Now you know good and well that ain't going to work." No time for proper English at a moment like this. It ain't going to work. Time went by, and I waddled more, and my stomach grew more, and my concern about the birth process mounted.

Back then, women still wore maternity clothes, and my belly was filling those maternity jeans, leaving little room for anything. You see, as large as my stomach was getting, I began to wonder how in the world this baby was going to be born. I had thought maybe a C-section. However, the doctor, in his spanking clean white doctor's hospital gown and shoes, said, "You don't need to have a C-section. You are quite capable of having a vaginal birth."

"What about something for the pain?" I responded, trying to keep hope alive.

"When the time comes, you will be given something for the pain." Somehow, his words did not really ease my anxiety. I shuddered as flashbacks of my first daughter's birth crossed my mind.

The day arrived, and I went to the hospital with my Mom, just like with my first daughter. My husband also must have been feeling the pangs of our first try at childbirth because he went to a bar to get a drink before coming to the hospital. By the time he got there, things had begun to get really uncomfortable. I had waited a little too long to get to the hospital. I was told I had just made it and would get the epidural to help ease the pain.

Everything was kind of a blur, but I do remember that moment when I heard, "I need you to stay still while we give you the epidural. You will feel a pinch, but you must stay still."

Squinching my eyes shut, trying to ignore, while being fully aware of the fact that my backside was totally exposed (I never get used to that). I tried to still my body and hoped I didn't move. Then, everything seemed to come into focus because it was time.

I had dilated the requisite nine centimeters. I was rolled down someplace to a room with very bright lights. Legs were put in those stirrups. My husband, in tow, looked concerned and helpless.

Well, here we go again. "Push," said the doctor.

"Push," said my husband.

Pushing was my job, and I pushed, but then I felt the pain. Oh, my goodness. "Do I need more medicine?" I queried in a shriek.

"We can't give you another one. You have had one, and it should be working."

I will not even write the number of times I remember just screaming. "Can you help me?" This was directed at my husband. "Why is it hurting if I had the medicine?"

At some point, that seemed like hours later, I remember my second daughter pushing her way into the world. The relief I felt was immediate.

They whisked her away to be cleaned up.

Some indeterminant span of time later, I was asked, "Would you like to hold your daughter?"

I weakly nodded, and she was placed in my arms. I am not sure how long I held her. I heard them giving her statistics. "She weighed in at 9 pounds 8 ounces.

"Wow," I sleepily uttered. "She's a big baby." And, then, I fell off to sleep, thanking God that she was here. I didn't forget the pain. I was just overjoyed at the birth of my beautiful daughter.

My second silver lining.

* * *

SILVER LINING THREE

For the second time, my shape had returned to pre-pregnancy size. I felt confident that the same would be true after my third birth. This time, I had survived an infection while I was pregnant.

"Everything looks fine," was the doctor's comment following my last exam.

Things were in shape at the house, and my Mom was more than willing to help me once the baby came home. So, I had no real concerns about bringing a third child into the world. Everything except that one recurring issue. Now, I am an optimistic kind of woman; I thought, "Well, the third time will surely be the charm. Right?"

Then those feelings returned, they began to creep into my conscious space, and my murmurings changed, "Two times you have done this, Liz. What are you thinking? Who are you fooling?" I waffled back to the positive. "At least we know we will have a boy. At least the sonogram says it will be a boy." I told myself, trying to stay positive, but my reality got the better of me.

"But you do know this is going to hurt." By this time, I was no longer fooling myself. At the end of this process, there would be pain.

I thought I had things together. "I'm not going to that hospital until it's closer to time for me to get the epidural. I won't get there too early. Then I won't get sent back home. I cannot get sent back home." This was going through my mind when I called my husband to let him know I was finally heading to the hospital. My husband had to work. I would learn later that he was blocked in and had to get someone to move so he could leave and meet me at the hospital.

I was already in some pain. My water broke this time. Everything is on track. At least, that's what I was thinking. We arrived at that hospital, and by now, the pain was pretty severe. As I'm being rolled up to the maternity ward,

I tell myself, "Just a little farther, and I'll be getting that medicine to stop this pain, and this delivery will go well."

"She's fully dilated." I do not know whose voice that was.

"Let's get her to the delivery room." I thought they must have forgotten their own process.

"What about the medicine? I haven't had the medicine." I said, almost panicking.

"You arrived too late for any medicine. You are ready to give birth."

"Hold up!! I need that medicine." Reality sunk in, and I needed this process to stop. But it's hard to take control when you are on a gurney, you have somehow been taken out of your clothes, your husband hasn't arrived yet, and you are in the midst of yet another contraction!!

So, I did the only thing I knew how to do. I screamed. I mean, I really screamed!

"You'll have to stop that screaming. You are upsetting the other patients on the ward."

"Give me some meds, and I'll stop screaming!" I bellowed.

"You are too far along to get the epidural. You will be having this baby naturally."

"Are you kidding me?! I need drugs."

I just screamed, and somewhere in the chaos, I heard "Push."

I was told it didn't take long for my son to be born. But I sure know it hurt like crazy. "Six pounds." I heard it, but I couldn't believe it. My smallest child hurt the most.

"We'll have to sew you up. He tore you. We'll give you something so we can sew you up."

"They have got to be kidding! Now they are going to give me something for pain?" I sarcastically said to myself. I never even felt the needle or the sewing.

After sewing me up, they handed me my clean little boy, and all was right with the world again.

* * *

NO, I HAVE NOT FORGOTTEN the pain. No matter what others say about how you forget the pain of childbirth, I have not. Sixty-three years later, I still shudder at the mere thought of labor and childbirth. I rarely enter into conversations about the birthing experience with new expectant mothers. I do not think ii is fair to share my horror stories. The thing that makes up for that pain is the joy my children give me. No matter what, I love those three kids. And you know what? If I had to do it over, I would just do it anyway because having a little (not a lot of) courage has given me three silver linings.

The Dream. The Dance.

I am spending time with my grandkids. I am listening as they share with one another what they would like to be when they grow up.

"I want to be a fireman or a policeman."

"I want to bake and draw."

"I don't know yet."

As they were chatting, I began to daydream and went back to a time when I, too, was so emphatically filled with pride as I announced to myself what I wanted to be when I grew up. A smile began to spread across my face as I closed my eyes. I was reminiscing about the innocent joy of a child forming a dream. My grandchildren's voices grew dimmer as I remembered the count, and heard the melody of the Skater's Waltz. I began to hum and sway:

One, two, three, one, two three, one, two three, one, two three, one, two three, one, two three, one, two three, one, two three, one, two three I see the steps: balancé, balancé, balancé, chaîné turn, turn. la, la, la, la, la, la, la, la, la, la, la, la, la, la, la, la.

Dancing! I want to dance. Yes, I want to dance! I will be a dancer!!

My cousin attended this dance school that practiced in a recreation center near the Southeast Washington DC home where she lived with her mom, dad, sister, and brother. One day, my Mom asked if my sister and I wanted to take dance lessons. We said yes.

So, we started going to dance classes with my cousin. We practiced and practiced. I thought we would be dancing in the first concert after we joined. However, we joined too late and could only attend the dance school's winter dance recital and sit in the audience. What a disappointment!

As I sat in my seat and watched what unfolded on the stage, my eyes grew wider and wider. I became mesmerized (okay, as mesmerized as you can be at four or five years old). I was so excited I could hardly sit still. The dancers moved across the stage in beautiful colored skirts. I would later learn that the shorter ones were called tutus. I saw little and tall dancers. And I told myself, "Wow, I think I want to do that!"

They moved to the Nutcracker Suite's Swan Lake and Émile Waldteufel's The Skater's Waltz.

The young girls were my age! Well, that confirms it! " Hum, I really can do this too!"

Many days after the concert, I would move around the house doing what I remembered. Step and kick, Step and kick. Singing "Dum, Dum, Dum." That tune seemed to be stuck in my mind. I seemed to glide with the music. Tchaikovsky still has a warm place in my heart. "Next year, I will be on the stage too!"

But it didn't stop with classical ballet. They danced to "That's What I Call Balling the Jack," "Candy Man," can cause he mixes it with love and makes the world taste good," and "Rocking Around the Christmas Tree at the Christmas party hop."

I do remember the first time I did tap dancing. The audience would clap after each dance routine. After my first recital, my Mom and aunt said, "The audience was clapping for you. Your tap dancing was great! You had such energy!"

I still beam at their compliments.

The music made me feel like I was floating in the air. My satin skirt and shining black tap shoes made me feel like I could dance. I can still see myself. Somehow, I had garnered a spot on the front row, all the way to the left of the stage.

Tap, tap, cross in back, tap, tap, cross in back. Toe tap, heel to the right, cross over toe tap heel with the left. Toe tap, heel to the right, cross over toe tap, heel with the left. Tap, heel. Tap, heel. Tap, heel. Tap heel.

Coming out of my musings, for a moment, a thought just came to me. You know, as a child, being in a performance was the only time I was allowed to wear makeup. Dreamily, I recalled, Yes, when I was on the stage, I could wear makeup. Our dance teachers told our parents it was necessary so the audience could see our faces from where they sat.

Drifting back into my musings, I saw the stage lights. Lights, camera action.

The stage flood lights are bright reds and blues, greens and yellows! They were so bright we couldn't see who was in the audience out there beyond the lights. That was probably good because we didn't have to be afraid of what we could not see. We ran out on stage, took a ballet seat on the floor, lowered our heads, and awaited the first lilt of the music. I was happy to be a part of the performing group, finally.

"Yes," I continued to nod. Once again, I allowed the music in my head to cause my body to sway from side to side with my eyes closed. I traveled deeper into the memory of how it all felt, seeing some of the movements forming in my mind, humming to myself.

"Wow, that waltz where we looked like snow fairies all dressed up in our white was dreamlike." We even wore white earmuffs and handmuffs. The older girls danced to "Go Tell It on Mountain."

Coming out of my revelry, I focused back on my grandchildren, and there seemed to be a lull in their chatter. Not missing a step, I said, "Yes, there was a time when I couldn't wait. And then there was total elation! I became a dancer. I knew that was what I wanted to be, and I did it. That was a long time ago when I was a little girl with a dream. That dream did come true. I danced for so many years, but that was where it began. So, you keep dreaming. You don't have to know now, but when you do figure it out, follow that dream.

They returned to their chattering, and after a while of listening, I drifted again; I hummed the Skater's Waltz as I drifted off to dream to sleep.

It Can Be Okay To Be Green

It's not easy bein' green Having to spend each day The color of the leaves When I think it could be nicer Bein' red or yellow or gold Or something much more colorful like that It's not easy bein' green It seems you blend in With so many other ordinary things And people tend to pass you over 'Cause you're not standing out Like flashy sparkles on the water Or stars in the sky But green's the color of spring And green can be cool and friendly like And green can be big like a mountain Or important like a river or tall like a tree When green is all there is to be It could make you wonder why But, why wonder, why wonder? I'm green and it'll do fine It's beautiful and I think it's what I want to be Lyrics of Bein' Green By Joe Repaso; retrieved from https://www.youtube.com/watch?v=KHR6HkHySWY

* * *

I can still see the picture that was taken of me all those years ago. I was sitting in a paisley printed leather upholstered chair against a wall between the living room and dining room of our small red brick semi-detached house.

I had a large smile on my face because I was waiting for my date. I was a thin teenager, and the dress I wore seemed to overwhelm my person. Nevertheless, I was pleased and ready.

But I've gotten ahead of myself.

It was the spring semester of 1978. This was my senior year in high school. It was the year I was to go to my high school prom. Only I did not have a date. So, I was feeling pretty green. Yes, Green.

Not blue, but green. You know, like the song "It isn't easy being green having to spend each day the color of leaves."

Rudy, on The Cosby Show, felt green because she couldn't wear her summer dress to a wintertime party.

Kermit the frog felt green because he felt he blended into the ordinary and wasn't noticed. I felt green because I did not have a date, and prom was fast approaching.

But my rescue was on the horizon!! I was part of the music major program and sang in the Female Chorus and Mixed Chorus.

The director of the Mixed Chorus also directed the Male Chorus. The Male Chorus had an annual Pageant to crown a queen. They voted me to be a member of the queen's court. To my benefit, they would not leave a member of the court to go to the prom alone. I am not sure how they found out. However, once they did, I was asked if I would mind going to the prom with one of the guys in the Chorus.

"No, I will go out with him," was my ready response.

So, my green brightened some. I figured it was a mercy date. But I was still grateful that they helped me get a date. The young gentleman who took me was extremely kind to do so. I am not even sure that he would have taken me if they had not asked him. I wasn't exactly what one considered the foxiest or prettiest girl in the 12th grade. Bottom line, I will always be grateful to him for his kindness.

To the reader or listener: No pity here. By the time I was in the 12th grade, I was okay with my looks.

Now, you might wonder why in the world I am writing about this when I'm supposed to be talking about the color green. Well, I'm getting to that now.

With a date for me all lined up, I had to decide what to wear. The other two ladies in our prom group already knew with whom they were going and what they would wear. I knew my parents didn't have much money to buy one of those fancy, ready-made dresses. So, another rescue came into view. My brother, who was a year behind me, was a member of the Male Chorus. He was also great at sewing. He could sew up an outfit without using a pattern.

"I got you. I will make your dress. Just show me what you want to wear."

"Thanks!! We were not huggers, but my beaming smile showed him how happy I was.

Looking through pictures in books and magazines, I came across one and said, "This is the one!" I picked out a hoop-styled dress like the ones they wore to balls in colonial days.

Off my Mom and I went to the store to get the materials to make the dress. I walked up and down rows and rows of material in every color of the rainbow. I turned and bathed myself in those elaborate spring colors—yellows, blues, pinks, and peaches. I touched different swatches of material and stopped when I saw and felt one that, to me, was the perfect one.

"Mom, this is the one I want." I had settled on a white eyelet material that stood out even amongst those other brilliant colors. The dress of my dreams would be white.

"Okay." My Mom responded after looking at the price per yard.

Because the eyelet design would have my skin peeking through the many tiny, intricate holes, I then turned to find something for the underskirt. Once again, I wandered through the colored fabric. I repeated the ritual of feeling the material and settled on light green pastel satin for the underskirt. I had the material and thread in hand. My Mom's nod of approval put a smile on my face, and we moved to the cash register. My Mom said, "We'll take these." She paid for my selection, and we returned home.

My brother set about making the dress I would wear to the prom. I did not watch over what he was doing. I just trusted that I would be pleased with his efforts. I had a date, and I would have a dress!

"What color are you wearing to the prom?" We were at school, and that was my prom date asking me that question.

Smiling inwardly and outwardly because he seemed to be happy about going with me, I replied, "I am going to wear green and white."

"Okay. I will match you. I will meet you at your home with the others in our group."

Assessing him, I noticed he was taller than me. I had not paid attention before. So, I will not be taller than he in my heels. That was a good thing!

Actually, I think my date was just as curious, nervous, and unsure as I was.

Prom day arrived. I had gone to the hairdresser and got my usual shoulder-length snatch back, which looked more like a many-layered flip-up hairstyle. My hair was mostly dark brown now because the majority of the red hair I had been born with had grown out. No makeup and no fingernail polish. My Mom didn't think we should wear makeup.

I looked out the window and saw him drive up in a dark green car. He walked to the door with a smile on his face that made him look very handsome. His dark green suit and light green shirt really made him debonair. My long white dress billowed out as best it could. My mom couldn't get me a corset or hoop skirt to make it stand up properly. But to me, the underskirt was perfect. That pastel green peeked through the eyelet on the white outer dress, and when I walked, the satin green color seemed to shimmer even more.

His dark green accented my satin pastel green. And he had one more asset to complement our ensemble. He presented me with a green and white wrist corsage. I was elated. My gown was not sleek like my girlfriends' gowns, but I was just happy to be in that green. My date and I wore coordinated outfits. Our clothes matched the car. I felt special.

So, I picked up my small black dress purse from the chair where my parents had taken the picture. And, by the way, that chair was upholstered in a floral print that was splattered with shades of green. So, for one fabulous evening, I was feeling beautifully accepted in green as the six of us headed out for our prom night.

The song Bein' Green ends with the words: "When green is all there is to be. It could make you wonder why. But, why wonder, why wonder?

I'm green, and it'll do fine. It's beautiful, and I think it's what I want to be."

Oh yes, the date ended with a light kiss on the lips– my very first kiss. So, it definitely can be okay to be green!!

When Euphoria is Healthy Happiness

To my children and my grandchildren:

I know I am always trying to find ways to encourage each of you to put your trust in God. Bear with me because this is another one of those times. Let me give you a few personal examples of how I have felt a direct connection with that higher power.

This story is written from my perspective, feelings, and recollection. I do not necessarily remember every word that was said and every descriptive aspect in each of these memories. However, I do remember how it felt and what it meant to me.

Sometimes in my life, I experience such a sense of emotional happiness generated by feeling a sincere closeness to God. For example, one day, on my way to work, I was riding across a bridge going from Southeast to Northwest. I peered out the front window of my car and saw a rainbow. Happiness invaded my entire being. That rainbow was so vividly beautiful. The colors just seemed to blend from one to another. That rainbow spanned the sky. I felt so peaceful and I knew for certain that God was nearby.

Another example is driving into my Waldorf, Maryland, neighborhood and having such an abundance of gratitude wash over me as I marvel at God's goodness to me because I never thought I would own a house or a car, and at 40, I was able to purchase both.

The timing of those two accomplishments sometimes makes my inward laughter bubble forth, especially when one of you seems to be in such a rush to achieve.

I gently want to remind you how long it took me to get to a point where I could relax and know that my steps had been and continue to be ordered in the right direction by the best guide.

Let me see if I can explain this better. You all know that in May 2023, I traveled to Indiana to participate in the hooding ceremony for my doctorate degree .

As part of that ceremony, the graduates were asked to come to the altar for prayer. Family members who were in attendance were asked to come and stand behind us and place their hands on our shoulders as a show of support for all we had accomplished that culminated in that day's ceremony. This symbolic gesture was also intended to assure us of their willingness to be our encouragers as we embarked on our ministry journey.

As the prayer unfolded, I felt my son's hands on my shoulder. It is almost impossible to put into words the feeling that washed over me. I began to feel at peace and to feel sheer happiness coursing through my body. I believe it was the Holy Spirit I felt moving through me and that room. We began to sing a song, and the music seemed to carry me even more to that spiritual place. I knew I was on the right path and that Jesus would be with me. Tears began to stream down my cheeks, and once again, I knew the peace that only a relationship with Christ can bring.

The hooding ceremony was not the first time I had felt that peaceful happiness. One day in 1998 or 1999, I was alone in the break room at work. It had been a busy morning. I decided to close my eyes and try to silence my mind for a few minutes.

I prayed a little, and then I just let my mind drift. The next thing I knew, I was floating outside of my body as if on clouds. I seemed to be in a place of complete peace. I could see the clouds and feel the calm. It was sheer blissfulness. I could see and feel, but nothing else came into my mind. I was present only in that place. Nothing, and I mean nothing, came to mind. It felt like I was sitting with God and enjoying the time together. When I left that euphoric space, I felt like my entire soul had been refreshed.

I have never had that complete mind-surrendering experience again.

Aa time came when I had achieved several milestones in pursuit of becoming a minister. It was after I had been licensed to preach, received my Master's in Theology, and passed the ordination exam. My church voted and approved my ordination. It was at that very point that I experienced another body-cleansing, soul-refreshing experience of God's Love. The year was 2011, the formalities had been completed, and my ordination service was scheduled.

At my ordination, songs were sung. Scriptures were read. Prayers were lifted. A female minister preached the sermonette. I swayed and sang, nodded, and occasionally said Amen. I was happy I had reached this point. The room was pregnant with a growing sense of spirituality. And I was brimming with the indwelling of the Holy Spirit.

Then, the part of the service came when the church's Deacons and other clergy present were asked to lay hands on me. A chair was placed before the altar, and I was asked to sit on that chair. I had seen this done before. It was nothing new to me. Or, so I thought. I was then surrounded by over twenty people who stretched out their hands to touch my shoulders and head. Music played in the background as the reverend of our church began to pray. I do not remember the words of that prayer.

I do remember being overwhelmed with emotion. I no longer noticed the weight of the hands pressing on my shoulders. I remember my happiness growing stronger and stronger. This happiness was totally different from the satisfaction of eating Butter Brickle ice cream or Recess' Peanut Butter Cups. This happiness was more powerful than holding each of my children for the first time. This was more soul-searing than marrying my husband or getting an "A" on a difficult test. If you wrapped all the great events that have happened in my life and rolled them into one great big ball of joy, it would not have surpassed the euphoria I felt on that day.

My shoulders shook, and my body seemed to go limp. I silently cried so hard that it became impossible to shield those tears from those who stood near me. It was as if I had no control over the joy that flooded my being. I was helpless and empowered at all at the same time.

It was at that point that I knew, not guessed or surmised. I knew that I had been called to serve God in ministry.

Almost 12 years later, I still get overjoyed when I think about my ordination day.

So, my children and my grandchildren do not look for euphoric happiness in earthly concoctions that poison the mind, body, and soul. Do not place so much stock in material things or be overly moved by human meanness.

If there is one thing I want to leave with you, it is the assurance that what I have in my heart and the love God gives me is real. These things are not for me alone. I am not part of some isolated group of people with a connection to God. You also have that connection. It is much more rewarding than anything you will find on Earth.

Seek that experience every day. Yes, seek that euphoric experience – happiness beyond that peace that passes understanding. Just as God is with me, he will be with you, too.

I did it anyway

Many times, I did it anyway. Indeed, my life is full of those "I did it anyway" moments. Maybe I'm a glutton for punishment. I do not know. Truth be told, I am not a daredevil. I do not enjoy taking chances. Yet, I find myself doing things anyway. An example of my tendency to do things anyway would be the two additional times I decided to get pregnant. As if I didn't vividly remember the pain involved the first time, I still did it again. But those pregnancy stories and their happy endings are captured in an earlier segment of these memoirs.

How did I get here?

The church was dimmed, and we were in the midst of our concert. I had been singing with the college Gospel Choir for a while now. We had sung at different churches in the area and were well received. Our choir had a very nice, rich sound.

Our director was a couple of years ahead of me. We grew up in Washington, DC, living across the street from each other. I didn't know he was there when I applied. Anyway, we became pretty good friends. While in college, we won disco contests as dance partners.

Back to the night in question. What led up to this moment of reckoning? I had become a little bothered by the fact that our director only asked one young lady in the choir to sing solos. She was going to sing two or three solos at the concert. Now, she had been singing solos at most of our engagements. No one else was ever asked if they wanted to sing solo.

One day, I had had enough and asked, "Why does she sing all the solos?" She didn't get upset. She and I were friends, so there was no meanness in my question. I just wanted to know.

"I didn't know anyone else wanted to sing. Would you like to sing one of the leads to a song?"

Okay, I had put my foot in it. I had sung most of my life. I sang a small part in a play in high school that ran for several engagements in "Ford's Theater" and the L'Enfant Plaza Theater. I sang small parts of songs in various choirs at my home church. But, up to that point, I never really sang a lead in a song.

"Yes. I would like to sing a lead." I said, even though I was not exactly sure I could pull it off.

The usual soloist offered to let me sing "Stretch Out." This decision was made a couple of days before the concert. So, I had to learn the solo with only a few opportunities to run through it, and then it was Sunday. It was the day of our concert.

I found myself standing behind a grand piano holding a microphone in my hand. The choir was behind me, and my director friend was tinkling the ivories.

Just before I began to sing, I looked out and saw one of my best friends. His tall 6-foot-5-inch slender frame and handsome face were like a beacon in the dimly lit room.

The director completed the song's intro. I began the first lyrics and sang the lead as the choir sang backup. The upbeat tempo flowed. With the microphone shaking in my hand, I belted that "Stretch Out" song with trembling bravado. The next thing I knew, the song had ended, and I was listening to loud applause.

Later, at the reception, my friends told me what a great job I had done. But they told me something else that I had not even realized.

"You really sang the right song." One of my friends said.

"Really? Why is that?"

"'Cause you sang 'Stretch Out' and were stretched out across that piano."

"What?" I incredulously asked.

My tall friend added, "Yep. You looked like you were singing Stretch Out in a jazz club."

I had to do a mental double-take and think. "Man, I was leaning on that piano, wasn't I?"

We all enjoyed a hearty laugh at my antics. I had made it through the solo, leaning on that piano for support. That was my first real solo. My stomach was full of bubbles. The feeling of singing God's praises has spiraled on from that point, and I have since had many opportunities to belt out some song or another. Each time my stomach is full of butterflies, my prayers get more fervent.

I love to sing. Nervous and praying fervently each time? Next time? I will just do it anyway.

Senses?

One of the most incredible things God has ever given me is the gift of sight. I am not thinking about perfect vision, because I wear glasses. For most of my life, without those glasses, my eyesight was blurry.

Even with blurry human vision, I have indelible images of days gone by that are stamped on my mind. These images embody all of the senses. The memories are so fresh that it is as if these events occurred yesterday. Even now, as I recall them, all my senses are ignited – visions of touching, seeing, hearing, smelling, and tasting.

* * *

It was 1988, and the atmosphere had been buzzing with excitement ever since the Redskins (now the Commanders), led by quarterback Doug Williams, won the Superbowl.

The Black community was overjoyed that a Black quarterback had done so well. The team has won, and Doug Williams had coveted the opportunity to make the famous statement, "I'm going to Disney World."

Everyone made preparations for that game. Super Bowl parties were planned throughout the city.

My Mom and Dad were no different. We made plans to have a house full of people over to watch the game. My husband and I bought Super Bowl sweatshirts. We even bought one for our firstborn, 1-year-old daughter. The sweatshirts had the Redskins symbol and Doug William's face, name, and number emblazoned across the chest. My little girl also wore gold sweatpants and little sneakers. She toddled around the house with her best friend and cousin, who was dressed in the same outfit. The two toddlers were not really aware of the game playing out on the television. Those two were just excited to have some freedom to roam.

Those were the days when everyone in the house would watch the children. If a child was about to toddle over, a pair of adults' hands would steady them. When the adults got a plate, someone made sure the children had a plate as well. So, as long as the kids were okay, parents could relax. We ate and drank as much as we wanted.

Each time our team did something well, the shouts of "Yeah!" and the high-fives and playful shoves had the house rocking. It was a grand time in that house, and when the game ended, we all sat around basking in the afterglow of the events that unfolded on that floor-model color television set. Doug Williams had thrown four touchdowns, and we had won by a score of 42-10. Yep, we were on cloud nine!!

"Anyone going to the game?" Someone asked.

"I want to go said my brother, who was a year younger than me.

"I have to work." That was my husband's response.

"I want to go," I said, and one of my family friends also wanted to go . We just felt so excited, and giddy, and gleeful that we had won that game. WE WON THE SUPERBOWL!! We were geared up to continue the celebration by attending that parade.

Sunday, January 31, 1988, ended on a high note!

* * *

THE DAY OF THE PARADE arrived – February 4, 1988. It was my daughter's second birthday. She was too little to come with us to the parade. We planned to have a birthday party for her the following weekend. My Mom had agreed to watch her.

Outside, it was a blustery day with the temperature in the 40s. We dressed in jeans, sweaters, and winter coats with hats and gloves. The government was closed, and the law firm I worked for on Pennsylvania Avenue, and many other businesses along the parade route were also closed. The streets began filling early with Washington fans who determined to be in town when the team appeared. It was reported that there may have been 600,000 people. Everyone was laughing and walking along. Children and adults were caught up in the happy spirit of the occasion.

There were tales of Superbowl parties, and you would hear someone say, "Did you see that touchdown?"

And someone with a voice filled with laughter replied, "Which one? He completed four."

Another group recalled their party menu – "We had ribs, chicken, potato salad, baked beans, and salad. The beer and other drinks were bottomless."

There was no hint of racial discord for just a moment in time. All sorts of people were just hanging out together, enjoying the sights, sounds, and smells of victory. It was just plain old-fashioned fun.

But then, in the midst of all that gaiety, my mood changed. I began looking around me and noticed there were *so* many people. It seemed sudden, but I could not see the street. All I could see was a whole lot of people's feet. I managed to keep sight of my brother and our friend, as we were being propelled along by that ever-growing throng.

I will not call them a mob. They were not. They were just as happy as they could be. There were just too many of us. As the crowd pressed in, my jovial attitude began to change to alarm. My emotions began pulling at one another. I tried to remain calm. After all, this was a momentous occasion.

We never seemed to stop moving. I began to lament the situation. We were propelled forward. At one point, we needed to get past a temporary fence that had been erected for the occasion. Our friend could not jump over the fence. So, we had to wait for her to find a way to go under. My brother and I jumped the barrier. You had no choice; you either jumped that fence or go under or around it. You could not stay there because everyone around you was trying to get to the point where our Super Bowl-winning team would greet us.

My feelings were just all over the place. I felt happy that the team had won, and that I had come to greet and celebrate with other fans.

But my heart was pounding, and I panicked at the sea of people that engulfed me. There was no exit. You had to go along with the crowd and hope for the best.

"Is this how the water feels when the waves act up, and there is a tempest brewing?" I said to myself.

Then, I realized I needed some heavenly help. So, I began to pray. "Dear Lord!" Not a quiet, softly rendered prayer.

This was a loud internal plea for help.

"Dear Lord! If you help me get out of this crowd, I will never go into another crowd like this!"

A few moments after that brief heart-ripping prayer, I heard a scream and watched as a woman with a baby in a stroller was trying to keep her child from being trampled. Luckily, the crowd heard her panicked voice and noticed. They must have heard because they began to stop pushing, and somehow, she was able to regain control of that carriage and move through the crowd. They just seemed to open up a path for her to pass through. But that path must have only been for her and her child because it closed up as soon as she moved through it. We once again were swamped by this group of celebrants.

I began breathing in an effort to take my mind off my surroundings. But then I heard someone say, "Someone just passed out."

The next thing I knew, I looked up, and a body was being passed along on the upstretched hands of the crowd. They gently passed her overhead to where someone had heard a first aid station was located. I am not kidding; they gently passed this woman over the crowd! It was surreal. It was such a beautiful thing to see.

We got close, but not close enough to be in front of the stage. Even though we did not see their arrival, the crowd's roar left no doubt that the team had indeed shown up.

We heard "Hail to the…" blaring through the outdoor speakers that lined the perimeter along the route. What we heard and saw was at a distance from center stage, but the atmosphere was pregnant with happiness.

We were still in a sea of people. I felt scared for myself but more fearful for those who brought their children to that parade. I still do not understand that decision. I felt thankful that I had left my young daughter at home.

I heard roars from that crowd that were louder than anything I had heard up to that point. The air was filled with smells of hotdogs and other barbecued items. The odor was so tantalizing that I conjured up the taste of a juicy hot dog and closed my eyes for a moment savoring that taste. It was so good. I had even had ketchup and relish on that imaginary hot dog.

For a moment, I forgot about the pressing people. Then, I was brought back to reality by the thought that I had no idea how anyone could get to any one of the vendors that day.

I do not remember how we got out of that crowd. However, I know I got out because I'm recounting this memory. We would not become aware of the fighting or other misconduct until it was reported on the news later that night. That was not a part of our experience, thank goodness.

It was one of the happiest and scariest days of my life. I still love the taste of a good hot dog. I still feel ecstatic when the Commanders win. I can still see those sweatshirts we wore. I love to hear the team fight song.

All of that joy, but needless to say, I continue to dodge any suggestion or invitation to be touched by another large throng of people.

All of my senses scream, "No more crowds!!" Long live the senses!!

Caution to the Wind

In high school, we were four girls who went about throwing caution to the wind.

Four young ladies. Why does it always seem to be four females? You know, like what is depicted in Sex in the City, Girl's Trip, or the Women. Anyway, the four of us did a daredevil stunts, tested fate, and tried our parents.

I remember one time we were going on a class trip to a movie. I cannot remember which movie it was. We went in a long brown sedan that belonged to the parents of one of my friends who was in the 11th grade. She was actually the only one of us who had a car.

I did not even have a driver's license at that point. There was no need for me to be in a hurry to drive because there were six of us; my older brother and sister already drove, and I did not feel like arguing over our parents' car.

Anyway, we high school girls were driving along at breakneck speed as usual. We took a ramp at top speed. We went around that ramp on two wheels, and we were all holding on with bated breath. We were too stupid to pray back then. So, we just rode in horrified silence as the tires whirred. She, seemingly more expert than her age indicated, held that wheel with a death grip, and somehow, she got that car to rebalance on all four wheels. We drove on to our destination at an understandably slower rate of speed. Although we did not say a word, the car was pregnant with our inner sighs of relief.

That's just one incident of us just being crazily normal teens who threw caution to the wind.

Another time, a group of us decided to ditch school. Yes, even me, a mother and a grandmother, Elizabeth Lynne Ellis (now Wiggins), had periods when she made unwise decisions that just seemed to be so much fun at the time!!

One school day, a bunch of us decided to go to a park and have a picnic. After eating our hastily put-together lunch, we decided to all take a "joy" ride together in a classmate's Volkswagen Bug. About 12 or 13 of us piled on top, on the sides, and inside that little egg of a car that should hold four or five at the most. Off we went for a joyride around the park. The car wasn't moving slowly either. Why is it that teenagers like to drive so fast? It was a bad idea because I remember the police showing up with sirens blaring.

"Pull over." We heard from the cop car's loudspeaker.

Our driver pulled over, and we jumped off and out of every inch of that Volkswagen. "Show me your license and registration." The policeman demanded from our driver.

"I don't have my license or registration with me." He replied.

Later, we learned that our driver was not old enough to have a license because he was only 14. "Oh man," is what I whispered while my other friends used terms that were a bit more colorful.

I guess the cop knew we were just out being pranksters. "Go back to school. You know you don't belong out here."

"What about my car?"

"The car will be impounded until your parents come and get it. You are lucky I don't run you all in for skipping school and piling on that car like that. Now go back to school!"

We dodged a bullet in another episode of high schoolers throwing caution to the wind.

Permit me to share one more caution to the wind episode. I got a call from my friends asking if I was going to the roller rink with them. We loved to go roller skating. My friend who had the car was an excellent roller-skater.

Now, I could skate to the music, do a gentle turn, and skate backward, but I did it all with much caution. But my friend could just sail at breakneck speed around that rink, kicking her leg up in the air as she extended into a turn that had her skating backward. She could leap and spin, duck and bend all while bouncing and snapping her fingers to the beat. Yes, she could really skate.

I would usually say yes right away to hanging out with my three friends. However, that evening, I knew I needed to get plenty of rest. I was scheduled to take the SATs the very next morning. The SAT is a very long college entrance exam. I needed to be alert to sit for it.

I was a pretty good student. I actually would graduate from high school with a 3.67 average. However, I needed SAT scores between 1338 and 1460 to get into Oberlin College.

"Should I go? I need to be ready for that test. Can I go and still get back home in time to be ready?" My internal tug of war went on like that for a while. The back and forth wind was howling in my mind as I sought ways to ignore caution and move toward the tempestuous pull of fun.

Into the phone, I said, "You all are coming right back home afterward? I must be in early tonight to get up and be alert when I go take the SAT."

"Yeah, the session ends at 10, so you should be home by about 10:30."

I did one more rapid mental questioning session: "Should I go? Well, she said we'll be home early." I can do it if I come home before 11." Teenager rationalization complete, to my friend, I replied, "Okay, I'm in."

"Great. "We will pick you up and head down the street. We picked up one more friend, and then we were on our way to the skating rink.

We were always up for a foolhardy challenge, and that night was no different.

With all four of us in the car, we headed toward the roller rink. We were on Marlboro Pike, in Maryland. The light ahead of us had just turned red. All it took was for one of us to say, "Hey, remember Happy Days when they jumped out of the car?"

The next thing I knew, the car was put in park. We all simultaneously opened the doors, jumped out of that brown sedan, and slammed all four car doors closed. We ran completely around the car, laughing and yelling, "One O'clock, Two O'clock, Three O'clock Rock..." all the way around. We opened the doors and jumped back in the car. We completed our game just in time for the traffic light to change. The car was thrown into gear, and off we sped. Now that I think about it, teen ladies can run pretty fast.

We did make it to the skating rink and had a great time. We skated in pairs. I did the general skate rounds, and the music was great. Bounce Skate boomed through the speakers. At different points, the lights were dimmed as the music slowed and the skaters coupled up. At other times during the session, the disco lighting bounced off the ceiling and floor, the beat picked up, and the skaters bounced around in time to the music.

Of course, by the end of the skate session, we skated so hard that we worked up an appetite and had to go to IHOP and get something to eat.

The momentum and gaiety of the evening made me forget I had a self-imposed curfew. I joined the others, and we laughed and ate pancakes until after 11:30. By the time I got home, it was after 12:30 the next morning. I tumbled into the bed, only half undressing.

I had my own personal human weekend alarm clock, and it sounded right on time. It was 6 a.m. "Get up, Elizabeth. You know you cannot be late for that test." That was my mother.

"Man, why in the world did I go out and forget I needed to get myself home early?"

I moaned my way up and must have brushed my teeth and washed my body because I do not remember smelling crazy. I threw on a pair of slacks and a shirt. Back then, I didn't wear jeans when I had something important to do. I combed my hair, ate something for breakfast, and dragged my drowsy body into the car that would take me to that exam.

The test was timed in six sections, testing our math, language, and logic competency through various questions and topics. I sat there with my number two pencil in hand. I do not remember much of anything on that test. I remember hearing a droning-on type of voice give test-taking instructions and give the initial permission to start. But I do not remember when they said to stop between sections. I do not remember if we had a break during the test. I remember feeling myself waking up from a deep sleep at one point.

"Time is up," I vaguely remember some voice saying.

I left that room thinking I had slept through the entire test. Now, you talk about making a very foolish decision!!! Caution to the wind!?

One day, a package arrived for me in the mail. From what was written on the return label, I knew my SAT scores were in that envelope. Then I began to bemoan the situation "Man, now I'm going to have to tell my parents I failed that test. They don't have money for me to keep taking this exam."

I braced myself for their disappointed looks. I opened that envelope and haltingly looked down at the rows of scores. To my surprise, I had passed that exam. I felt a smile slowly spread across my face as I realized I had scored high enough to get into Oberlin College!

Now, for the most part, each time I unwisely threw caution to the wind, things turned out okay. Well, scoring enough for Oberlin was actually wonderful!! Yes, those episodes had happy endings.

However, I hope the larger message received is that perhaps we all should make wiser choices before we go off and throw caution to the wind!

Habits

"Put your tongue in your mouth." I would hear my Mom say.

I am not the only person out there with habits. As a matter of fact, you know there are many people out there with habits. I would go so far as to say that everyone has at least one habit. Some suck a thumb. Others twist their hair. Then there are those who shake a leg so hard it bounces everything around them.

A habit is said to be cute when you are a child. But the older you get, the more folk like to remind you that you are too old to do that. Or, they have these age-old remedies that will cure you of that unseemly habit that has followed you throughout your life. You know, all the life you have lived up to turning the wise old age of four or five.

Then, one day, you decide it is best to try to hide your habit and only do it when you are in your private space.

Even after making that determination for secrecy, you still sometimes slip and do it again in public. Then you have to suffer those humiliating comments again. Folk do not know how hurtful they can be. They make you feel less than others, and for what?

My habit? I do not know when it started. I only know it has been with me for as long as I can remember. Everyone seemed to have something to say about it.

"Buzzie, your tongue is out." One of my aunts would remind me using that name she loved to call me.

"Stop poking fun at me," I would shriek at my brother, who was walking around poking his tongue out, mimicking the way he thought I looked. In my young mind, I thought he was probably doing it right, and it made me feel sick inside.

"Ouch," I shrieked.

My Mom had pinched me and said, "Didn't I tell you to stop sucking your tongue?"

"You want me to put some pepper on your tongue?" An aunt asked me. Then she told my Mom and Dad, "You should put pepper on her tongue. That's how I got him to stop sucking his thumb."

"Look at her. Look at Elizabeth. Your tongue is out." A classmate pointed at me and laughed so everyone within earshot could hear and see. They laughed and laughed. I cried and cried. It wasn't something I could help. I wasn't even aware I was doing it until someone pointed it out. It just felt comfortable to me.

I did it mainly when I was concentrating on something. I could be reading, and my tongue would come out. I could be watching TV, and there it would go again. Playing with a toy. Walking down the street. Sitting in class. It didn't matter when I let my guard down; my tongue would shoot out of mouth and rest against my lower lip. Of course, if I fell asleep, it was an automatic occurrence. Whenever I woke up, my tongue would be out. Sometimes, it felt like I would bite it off because my teeth would clamp shut, and I was unaware of what was occurring. Nothing and no one could stop it.

Now, this "habit" was caused because my tongue is quite long. Yes, I can touch my nose with my tongue. That is just how long it is.

My Mom and Dad thought the dentist might be able to help. So, they told them about it. That doctor told my parents, with me in the room, that they could break my jaws, clip my tongue from the back, and reset tongue in my mouth. I would be wired up for about six months. I could then wear braces to straighten my teeth.

I was in elementary school, for Pete's sake!!

So, I left the dentist with nice clean teeth and the habit of sucking my tongue still in place.

Sometimes, even friends would make fun of me. They had no idea that it was not funny and really hurt my feelings. But I never said anything to those friends. I just took it in stride and did all I could to be as cautious of it as possible. I went to great lengths to keep from doing this thing in public. It was hard to nap around others because I was afraid my secret would be revealed to a new crop of *merrymakers*.

I was in the library reading a book and would literally shake myself because I caught myself sucking my tongue! "There I go again."

Sitting on the bed watching TV with my fiancé, I was combing my hair. Out jutted my tongue. It was just like when I was a little girl combing my doll's hair.

At the age of 24, I lamented the fact that I still had shaken my tongue shaking habit. I shook myself, put my tongue in my mouth, and prayed my husband to be hadn't seen me.

I can laugh now because I had become a closeted-tongue-sucking woman. I did it as a tiny girl; I did it as a teen. I did it as a young adult. I do it as a senior citizen. I did it at different points yesterday. And I have done it several times while writing this piece.

Here's an amusingly interesting thought. During Covid, I found a bit of relief. As long as we had to wear masks, I could relax. Everywhere I went, I was safe and felt at peace. I had that sense of comfort. You see no one, and I mean no one, could tell if I happened to slip and allow myself to suck my own tongue. Imagine that!! It was as if my world had been opened to a new reality. I would catch myself sucking my tongue and just smile as I tucked it back between my lips. It did not matter whether I knew you or not. I could concentrate. I could enjoy my life. No one knew, and so it did not matter.

Now, believe me, I am thankful that Covid has abated quite a bit. However, my comfort once again became more challenging. My temporary cover was gone. That's okay. I could get used to it again. I just had to return to the old way of trying not to let this habit publicly rear its ugly head.

For those of you who believe you can break a person of a habit that gives them comfort, I am a witness to the fact that you cannot. You see, it is not something we do to make you feel embarrassed for us. It is not because we want to make you laugh or give you material for your amateur comedy act. It is not something we even really want to do. It is something that we do subconsciously.

It is 2024, and I will be 64 years old in November. I'm sitting here editing this piece and, several times, have caught myself sucking my tongue. And if it gives me peace and isn't hurting me or anyone else, you should be okay with it.

I am aware and okay with my habit, at least for the most part. There are still those moments when I am around other folk. And that old feeling returns. But then I settle down and think about all those people who know and love me and could not care less that I suck my tongue. I still get a little embarrassed, but it's okay. I shake it off and go ahead with life. And then, the world is okay with me again.

I pray that by sharing my story, others will be free from the torture that comes from having a habit that others do not understand or like. If you have a habit like mine, just tell folks, "It is another part of who I am.

To everyone else, I say, do not make your habit one that causes others shame. Remember, we all have habits!"

Tales of Two First Days of School

When I wrote this, I would turn 64 years old on November 27, 2023. And I still get excited on the first day of school.

I cannot remember when I was unhappy about going to school. I may have been nervous if it was my first day in a new school. But I always had that happy exhilarating feeling about the beginning of school. My heart races, and I begin to think about what I will wear and what I will learn.

When I was about to go the high school, I looked at transit maps and planned my route. I looked at the school's room layout and teacher assignments to see if I could visualize where my class would be in the building. Who will be in my class? I can't wait to see what books will be on my class syllabus.

The first day of my senior year in high school dawned full of promise. I now knew what classes I would have. For the third grade in high school, my homeroom teacher was the same one I had for the tenth and eleventh grades. My homeroom classmates would all be the same.

Seniors have that air of big men and women on campus. I was no different. That senior year, even wearing one of the two new outfits I bought, spoke volumes of my class status; at least they did to me. Glasses in my pocket, my tan flair-legged pants matching vest, and my bell-sleeved wine-colored shirt were pressed and neat.

I stepped off the W-4 public bus and walked with purpose across the street, and the football field, and into the building. I looked toward the escalator, noticed all the faces I recognized, and wasn't concerned with those I didn't know. After all, I was an upperclassman.

I nodded my head in approval and said to myself, "This is it. I'm here!"

* * *

One would think my feelings about school and the first day would rub off on my offspring. However, this was not the case for my beautiful oldest granddaughter. She went out with one of her great aunts and purchased several new outfits for the beginning of school so she would not have more choices than to wear her old clothes from her 11th grade year. She was entering that coveted grade – 12th grade – her senior year! How could she not be excited and over the moon at what this year would hold?

Over the moon could not have been further from her truth. Other than the new outfits, she was very nervous about returning to school.

"Grandma, I don't want to go to school. I would rather do homeschool."

"You will be fine. You will be able to get through this year."

This was really a reality check for me! I came face to face with one who did not enjoy the prospect of attending school.

"You know they fight all the time. They yell in the cafeteria. You know I did not eat in the cafeteria last year."

"Where did you eat?"

"In a teacher's classroom. So, I would not have to eat in the cafeteria."

"Okay."

"I don't like riding that bus. There is always something going on, and there needs to be more room. Some people do not get a seat."

"Well, remember you will not be riding the bus this year? I will be taking you and picking you up from school."

"Yes. I remember. You will pick me up after school."

"Yes. We must find out what time you get out of school."

"Yes, I have to take five classes!" "Yes, but you get out early."

"Okay. We can find out when I get out. I don't know if I will need lunch. But I will take my lunch anyway. My granddaughter said as she looked at her lunch bag. "This bag is dirty. I don't want to take that. I'll take a grocery bag."

"No. Your grandpop is off tomorrow; you can use his for one day, and we will get one for you before tomorrow."

"Okay, that will work." She said as she took the royal blue lunch bag and sat it on the kitchen table, ready for her to pack her lunch in the morning.

She laid out her clothes for the first day. A pair of black jeans, a nice button-down shirt, and her new black Converse high-top tennis shoes. She had a nice pair of black circular earrings to wear as well.

She went to bed still a little edgy but clear about what she would wear, the pocketbook she would carry, and the lunch she would eat.

The following day dawned.

"Good morning!" I said in the cheery voice I used to greet my children when I woke them when they were in school.

"Urr" was her soft response. "I'm sleepy. Can I rest a little more?"

"No. I have to get you to school on time and get to my swimming exercise class on time. Come on, let's go."

She continued to lie there, so I pulled the covers off and began tickling her feet.

"Grandma! I'm too old for that."

"No, you are never too old for that. But you are too old for a swat on your bottom." I laughingly said.

She stretched her beautiful long torso and rolled out of bed. She went into the bathroom, where she stayed for an eternity.

She finally came out of the bathroom, freshly showered, teeth brushed, and wearing the outfit she laid out the night before.

She also wore a lightly colored shade of lip gloss. Not too much, just enough to show she was a young lady about to "be a young adult." That was the one thing she was happy about. She would be a young adult, and 9th, 10th, and 11th graders were not about to be young adults.

After gathering her lunch, pocketbook, sketch pad, notebook paper, and a spiral notebook with pens and pencils, she joined me carrying my swim gear, and we got in the car to take her to school.

"Grandmom?" "Yes?"

"I'm nervous about going to school. I do not know who will be in my class. I do not know who will talk to me. I don't know when I get out of school."

"We will figure all of that out when we get to school. That's why I am with you. I will not leave until I know when to pick you up."

"Okay," she said quietly.

"I will go in with you."

As we approached the school, I looked at her, and she still seemed a little forlorn. To take her mind off things, I asked her, "Can you tell me where to turn into the lot? I sometimes forget where to go,"

"Okay. Don't go in the first driveway. That is for buses."

"Okay. Not this one?"

"No, the next one."

We drove along, and I turned into the second entryway. Still wanting to be sure it was her choice, I asked her, "Do you want me to go in with you?"

"Yes."

"Okay." I pulled up and asked the person directing traffic, "I need to go in with her. Can you tell me where I can park?"

"Yes, just drive over there and park," he said as he pointed to a parking lot just a few feet from where we were sitting.

I parked the car, and we went to enter the school. "Parents have to enter through that door just over there."

We followed directions and entered the school through the correct door. We went into the main office. We approached the desk, and I said, "My granddaughter gets out of school early, and I need to know what time I should pick her up."

"Will you be getting her every day? If she gets out early, she cannot stay around the school."

"Yes, I will pick her up every day. That is why I need to know what time she gets out."

"Let me check her schedule."

My granddaughter gave her name, and the assistant looked it up. "She will get out at 12:07 this week. She must check her weekly schedule to see if the time changes. Let me show you how to look it up." She said to my granddaughter.

After seeing how to look up the time her day would end, we turned to leave the office. We headed down the hall.

"I do not know where to go." She said.

My granddaughter thought I would be able to go to class with her. However, that is not how it is done in high school. A school worker in the hall said she would show my granddaughter where to go. "Your homeroom is right over there."

Once she realized I could not go with her, she scooted off quickly toward the class the worker had indicated.

I smiled, turned, and left the building, satisfied that I had at least gotten her to the building for her first day of school.

"Grandma, are you in the parking lot?" That was the text I received around 11:30.

"No, I'm not there yet. But I am on my way. I will be there when you get out of school."

"Okay."

About 15 minutes later I received another text. "Where are you going to park?"

"I will be right at the door where you went in."

Five minutes later, "Are you where the buses are?"

"I am parked right in front of the door that says Main Office where we went in. this morning"

"Okay."

She came out of the building at 12:07. She got into the car and said, "Hi."

"How was your day?"

"There were a lot of people. They were everywhere. There were more people than last year. The cafeteria would be very loud. I do not like it when there are so many people."

"But you made your way through all the people and now you are out here, so we can now go home, right?"

"Yes!"

"And you did not have to go to the lunchroom because you got out before lunch."

"Yes!"

"So, you made it! You did very well on your first day of school! Let's go home."

Two very different reactions to the first day of school. Both reactions are very real. Both mattered to the one experiencing the day. I'm a little sad that my granddaughter did not experience the joy I did. But I plan to help her blossom, validate her feelings, and assure her that I will be there to support her.

Nevertheless, I am still excited about my granddaughter's senior year!

It Was Important Then and It is Important Now!

Bonjour! Bonjour! Mon nom est Elizabeth. J'etais soixante ans. J'adore la langue française!! (English: Hello! Hello! My name is Elizabeth I am 60 years old. I Love the French language!!)

I began taking French in the seventh grade. I loved my French teacher! Even though it was over 50 years ago, I remember my first French class as if it were yesterday....

Classe. Attention, classe. Bonjour!.

Bonjour was the first word I learned. But, no, after thinking about it, class in French is spelled c-l-a-s-s-e. So, 'class' was the first French word I learned, and 'Bonjour' was the second.

Our teacher would hold up an object and ask in English, "What object is this?" She would then repeat the question in French, "À quoi ça sert?"

"A pencil!" we all would shout in English.

"Bon, classe Pencil—le crayon." She said as she wrote the French word on the blackboard beside its English equivalent. "Repeat after me. Répètez après moi. Le crayon."

"Le crayon," I said with the rest of our class. In my mind, I told myself, "Répètez means repeat!" understood that French word!

From that day on, a new world was opened to me, and I had found a new love. From seventh through 12th grade, I took French every year. I loved it and felt like I was learning more and more with each passing year. I beamed at my report cards because I always had a lovely capital "A" beside my French course. By 12th grade, I was doing my head-body, shoulder-swaying dance in my seat as I peered down at that coveted "A."

The time came for me to apply for college, and I knew immediately that I would be signing up for French. I looked at the courses and decided I was beyond the beginner and the intermediate class levels.

I read the description of Advanced French and convinced myself that I was supposed to be in that class. Satisfied with my choice, I filled out my class schedule and handed it to the lady assisting with class registration.

The registrar assistant peered at my class form and then up at me and smiled as she asked, "Are you a freshman?"

"Yes," I beamed back. "This is my first year."

She tilted her head and gazed at me momentarily before saying, "Okay. These are the classes you want? I will have them entered in the system, and you will be all set."

I wondered if that look was meant to tell me I should think about my choices. I shrugged it off after a few seconds and moved on to get my meal ticket.

On the first day of my French class, and I entered and made my way to a desk that was placed in the semi-circle. I did not know anyone there. I kept my elation tucked away inside. But I was happy! Several other young ladies and men entered the room and likewise took a seat. The professor entered the classroom right at 10 minutes after the hour. The time was significant because we only had to wait for a professor for 10 minutes before leaving the class.

I had no desire to leave. I was excited about beginning that class.

As the door shut, he began to speak, "Bonjour classe. Bonjour classe!"

We all settled down, turned our eyes to the debonaire-looking professor, and fell silent as he continued to speak:

"So far, so good!" I told myself.

"Let me greet you in English. This is the only day that we will speak English in class. "Welcome to each of you. This is advanced French. First thing we are going to do is to allow, each of you to share something about what you did over the summer with the class. And yes, you may share in English."

I wonder if he noticed the look of relief on my face. "What did he say?" I asked myself. "*The only day we will speak English in class? What happened to saying it in English and then saying it in French?*"

I missed what a couple of my classmates were sharing about their summer escapades. Surprised by that revelation, I opened my textbook. "*Oh my goodness! This textbook is all in French; even the instructions were in French!!*"

I snapped out of it as I heard a classmate say, "We spent our summer in France this year. My dad had to work from the Paris office again, and we got to go with him."

"*Again!*" I internalized.

"I went to France for a couple of weeks just to hang out." Another shared.

Then it was my turn...

"I spent my summer at home in Washington, D.C., babysitting for a family friend," I murmured just loud enough for the class to hear me. To myself, I said, "*I think I'm out of my league in here.*"

I only supposed this to be true until my professor began again after the last person shared.

"Ladies and gentlemen, you learn French by speaking French. So again, I say welcome! Now. Maintenant, Je suis le professeur de français. Bienvenue. C'est du français avancé. J'espère que vous êtes heureux d'être ici. Dans cette classe, nous ne parlons pas anglais. Tout sera parlé en français. (English: I am the French professor. Welcome. This is Advanced French. I hope you are glad to be here. In this class we do not speak English. Everything will be spoken in French.)

J'ai des questions auxquelles j'aimerais que chacun d'entre vous réponde. Tout d'abord, comment dit-on son prénom en français ? Deuxièmement, quand est ton anniversaire ? Troisièmement, depuis combien d'années étudiez-vous le français ? où as-tu étudié le français ?(English : I have questions that I would like each of you to answer. First, how do you say your first name in French? Second, when is your birthday? Third, how many years have you been studying French? Where have you studied French.)

I sat there listening, captivated, mystified, and horrified.

The class began answering. I had no idea what he had asked. He had an accent and spoke rapidly. My teachers in the past spoke slowly. Suddenly, I realized that my teachers were teaching us by allowing us to depend on a crutch. They would talk in English when necessary. Here I was in a class where we had no such crutch. We had to speak French! Imagine that!!

I don't know why God decided to help me that day but thank you! I did not have to answer the teacher's questions. You know that show "Saved By The Bell?" Well, I was literally saved by the bell. In college, when that bell rings, you get to go. I had dodged a bullet. I did not have a clue what was said in that class. But I did have a clue as to what I would do next.

I immediately left that classroom and made a beeline to the Registrar's Office. I stood in that long first week of school, changing, adding, dropping classes line, waiting for my turn to plead for mercy. My turn arrived, and I went up to the registration counter.

"Good afternoon. (I remembered you always needed to be polite.) I need to change a class. Can you assist me, please?" (More politeness.) I then focused on the person I was asking for assistance and realized it was the same lady who had signed me up for my classes.

"Which class would you like to drop, and which would you like to add?"

Now I wonder if she remembered me. I could have imagined it, but it looked like she tilted her head and slightly nodded. Nevertheless, with as much bravado as possible,

I replied, "Would you please drop my Advanced French class and sign me up for Beginning French?"

I can laugh now, because it mattered then, and it matters now.

* * *

Several months before I turned 60, my son came to me and said, "Mom, I need you to take off from work so that you can be with me for a procedure I have coming up in the Fall."

"Okay, sure, son. Of course, I will be there with you." I put in a leave request to take off work, telling my supervisor what I needed to do.

My son held up that story until a few days before my 60th birthday party. He even helped me plan that party.

The party was the day before Thanksgiving, Wednesday, November 27th. That is when he finally admitted to me that he wasn't having a procedure but that he was taking me to Paris for my 60th birthday. He had an entire trip planned.

"I had to tell you so you could pack some clothes to go."

It was November 28, 2019, and I was about to leave for Paris, France! I never thought I would see Paris. I went to Thanksgiving breakfast at my church, and that night, I boarded a plane for France.

I still say it over and over because I could not believe it. I just never thought I would get to France. My parents had no money to send me on the foreign exchange program while I was in college. So, I continued to love the language and take classes whenever I could. But I had accepted the reality that I would never get there.

And there I was, taking pictures before the Eiffel Tower, walking through Paris crosswalks, and cruising down the Seine. Crossing the Champs-Élysées to take a picture before the Arc de Triomphe.

My son wanted to get a new pair of running shoes. So, I even tried out my French and spoke to a Nike store Salesman! I'm here. I can understand what the French say when they speak to me slowly. I admired and was even a little envious of the native speakers on the television who spoke très vite ! (English: very fast!) All those years. That embarrassing first day of college French! By my senior year in college I had Discovered I could carry on a conversation in French with my professor! All that!! And now I'm here!!

It mattered then, and it matters now! I love French!

Learning to Love Liz

Sunday, August 6, 2023. I Zoomed into Sunday school class. We were discussing Galatians 5. We had gotten to verse 14, which says to love others as yourself. This scripture has always caused me to pause and think about loving others as yourself. So, I offered up my thoughts for the class's consideration.

"What happens if you do not love yourself? If you do not love yourself, then just how are you going to treat me?"

I don't know if they understood what I was saying. Do you ever wonder whether those who mistreat you or do you some injustice or disservice, like themselves? Perhaps they are mean to you and me because they do not love themselves and are actually treating us the way they treat themselves.

My spiritual self takes this notion of loving self a step further. We really have to love ourselves the way God loves us. Then I asked myself, "Where in the world would I be if I had not learned how to love myself through the eyes of God? After all, I am an entire body, and I had to learn to love each and every part of me. Especially the parts family, friends and foes ridiculed at every opportunity." Maybe a step-down memory lane will bring this idea of loving oneself into better focus.

Eyes. We all have two of them. In another piece, I wrote about my battle with eyeglasses. So, I will not go deeply into that again. I will say that I had to find a way to love myself despite the glasses. As a little girl, I would take off my glasses and tell myself, "I look better." I went through school, even through college, thinking I looked better without my glasses. In college, I still looked at myself in that mirror, "Without the glasses, I think I look better. With the glasses, I think I am starting to look better." On and off those glasses went. "It does not matter," I finally said defeatedly. What peaked out from behind those lenses lead to me getting a boyfriend. I was never going to be the one getting asked to dance. I just have to deal with the way I look and accept that my eyes weren't anyone's idea of pretty."

Hair. My hair was not long, nor was it thick. As a little girl, it was reddish brown. I had to wear braids – two of them going down my back and two braids crossing my forehead for bangs. When I started wearing curls, my mom let me wear my hair curled in a flip or in an old lady style with waves all over my head. I think I looked pretty crazy and assumed others did, too. The one time my hair looked decent was when I wore a natural; an afro. I loved my bush, and it was always neat. At night, I would braid it, put rollers on the braids, and pick it out in the mornings. Didn't help much, though. I had plenty of friends. But still no boyfriend.

One thing about hair is that you can always add hair, dye it, and cut it.

But what happens when one day it falls out and will not grow back? That's precisely what happened to me. My hair came out in clumps in my late forties or early fifties. It would not grow back, and it was too short to add hair. I had to come to grips with the fact that my hair was what it was. Accepting it was a process. At first, I went around wearing a hat or a scarf. I would not allow my hair to be seen. I didn't like wigs because they made my head hot!! My hair eventually began to grow again. While hair was not my strong suit, I did come to appreciate and love my hair.!

Mouth. Look at Elizabeth," some mean boy would call out. "She looks like a monkey." The boys would laugh. Some of the girls would laugh, too. My friends did not laugh. "This is how she looks," my taunting peer would continue. He would push out his lower lip and puff out his cheeks.

Again, the kids would laugh. I would just move away or think about punching somebody. "Why do they always find something to make fun of? My tongue is too long for my mouth. So, it pushes my lower teeth out. So, my mouth is messed up." I tell myself over and over again. My mouth just doesn't help at all!! Took a minute to learn to love myself with the mouth I have.

Feet. I love dancing. However, dancing does not make for pretty feet. The hours of squeezing my feet into toe shoes for ballet, tap shoes for tap dancing for hours, and spinning and stomping through modern dance routines caused my toes to have white spots on the knuckles. My feet did not hurt unless I wore heels all day at work, danced the night away, and got up the next day and put on more heels to wear back to work. Then, they would get tired and hurt. But pain was not the problem. My feet looked injured. So, I stayed away from wearing sandals in the summer. If I found a pair of sandals I dared to wear, they had to cover the spots on my toes. I kept seeing commercials about pretty feet. I heard men talking about rubbing their ladies' feet. I was not going to show my feet to anyone. I wore socks all the time. For a time, I even wore socks to bed. At one point, I bought some foundation makeup that matched my skin and put makeup on my toes to cover the spots. My feet were just another thorn in my mind.

Calves. Even calves can create tension. That dancing I loved so much also made my calves large. After a teenage outing to buy boots, I knew again that I was different in an unhelpful way:

"Here are the boots you wanted to look at. We do have them in your size."

I took the boots and smiled as I felt the leather. I looked at them on the store dummy and nodded at how sleek they looked going up to just above the knee.

"Thank you," I smiled at the saleslady. But my smile slowly turned to a frown as I pulled the boots on. That beautiful boot stopped just at my calf. It would go no higher. My calf was just too big. Now, the same calves that others said made me look like a runner or were beautifully shaped were causing me to feel like my calves were ugly. No help to be had in the calves area!

Hands. "I am so sorry, but we must try a larger ring." "My goodness, these gloves usually fit every woman. We do not have them in a larger size." I looked at others' nails, and they looked so neat. I asked a friend, "Do you go to get your nails done?" No. I do them myself. My friend did not have to do anything with her nails. Well, I try, and my nails never look nice. For example, because I was going to a wedding, I went to the nail salon the other day. I had a manicure and a pedicure. The man took good care of me, and I thought my hands and feet looked nice.

He had to clip my nails down because they were different lengths. But that was okay. The day after getting them done, I saw pieces of skin sticking up around the manicure he had so painstakingly given me. My nails held up until after the wedding I attended, and then they went right back to looking crazy. So, much for pretty nails let alone pretty hands!

Waist. My waistline has never been great. Of course, I have had children. But even with a small waist, it never did what it should, and I could not effectively wear waist-lined clothes. Well, that's all I can say about a waist I do not have.

Body size. As a young child, I had long arms that hung below my knees. As a young adult, I would have the bulge of a baby, lose the baby fat, and repeat the cycle. Now, I have what they call a menopausal belly. Really! My waist changes so often that I have clothes from size 9 to 20. I keep them all so that I can still have something to wear, no matter my body size.

I am now laughing out loud at myself and my hysterical antics. I shamed my own body. I mean, think about it, Liz. Someone, including yourself, has had something negative to say about your entire body! Man, you could be a total wreck!!

And that brings me back to the idea that you have to love yourself through the love of God. It is the love that God has for me that makes me feel beautiful. It's not a word I would have used to describe myself as a younger me. But the more I bask in the love of Jesus, the more I love my body, my face, and all that I am inside and out. Yes, sometimes, I allow that flesh to pull at my heart, but I am quickly drawn back to knowing I look beautiful to God.

Now that I think about it, with all the things I complain about myself, my husband still saw and chose me. And he has never told me I was ugly. After all, what am I saying about him – that he fell in love with an ugly woman? What am I saying about the God I serve? I mean I do believe he makes no mistakes. So, I just bask in the love that I receive and feel beautiful every day.

And, because I love myself with the love of God, I can be open to loving others the way I love myself.

The Way It's Got To Be? Body & Soul!!

I have experienced the beautiful blending of body and soul many times. When I am on a path and working toward being my best self through the indwelling of Jesus Christ – body and soul, it is an amazing thing. When I have the opportunity to minister through music, it is literally like feeling the spirit moving through me. It is that moment when I know my ability to sing has been perfectly blended with God's amazing ability to turn my ordinary talent into a God-given gift. I feel as if my body is taken over, and what is heard is truly God moving within me.

When I dance, my soul envelopes my body so sweetly that my movements begin to interpret the music in a way that only comes when God unites the two in harmonic rhythms. Likewise, when I preach a sermon, I feel deep down in my soul that my words have reached someone. Once again, that same sense of peace envelopes me, and it is another miraculous combination of body and soul.

However... Yes, there always seems to be a however in my life. However, there are also times when I miss the mark in seeking a better way of life. At those moments, I fail to live up to even the lowest level of living a well-blended body and soul existence. One moment in time comes to mind.

I cannot remember the exact year. I know it was well before I met my husband in 1984, but I am not quite sure whether I had graduated from college. I am pretty certain it occurred before I went to live in New York City in late summer of 1982. I was still living in our family home in Southeast Washington, DC. I might have been home for summer break.

I still did not have a driver's license. I would guess this was sometime between 1978 and 1982. It was a time when we still jumped double Dutch, went roller skating, compared Donnie and Marie and the Osmonds to the Jackson Five, and danced to James Brown and Funkadelic.

It was when we understood in DC that slow dancing was a completely different dance at our parties because couples "slow dragged". Imagine the girl placing her leg between the boy's leg and the boy placing his between the girl's leg. The boy had his arms around the girl's neck, and the girl had her arms wrapped around the boy's waist. The tightly bound couple would rock back and forth and side to side and every now and then take a deep knee-grinding circle before rising to straight legs and beginning the synchronized routine again. This went on to the tunes of the Stylistics, Barry White, the Blue Notes, and Gladys Knight. It was a time when I sat on the side bobbing to music as I watched the others dance.

Families gathered on holidays and did not call it a family reunion. Just easy days of fun and mischief. Okay, enough going down that part of memory lane and back to this memory.

I had gone out to a cookout with family and friends. This was one of those cookouts at someone's house with plenty of food and drink. An event where those gathered were shooting the breeze, talking smack, chowing down on all sorts of good food, dancing to the music, singing on and off key to the soulful melodies that filled the air, and just having a good old-fashioned time of fun.

At these partying moments, there was generally a generous supply of alcohol, and the drink selections were many. The blender would be whirring as frozen daiquiris were made throughout the day. There would be rum and whisky and wine coolers and vodka, beer, and Kahlua. Of course, there would be soda, water, and juice for those who fancied non-alcoholic beverages or the ability to switch back and forth.

This was my "enjoying life" and "drinking to party" phase of life. So, of course, I bobbed my head in agreement with myself – I had to imbibe and enjoy myself. As the day turned to night, the singing, dancing, and drinking continued. You know, when you drink, it doesn't faze you a bit to dance by yourself. So, I danced and danced and drank.

Oh yes, did I forget to mention that I only enjoy drinks that taste like Kool-Aid? So, I seemed to forget that the alcohol was blended in those concoctions I poured down my throat. Anyway, when it came time to go home, I felt I had done a good amount of dancing and had just enjoyed myself. The glow I felt was partly the great crowd and partly the drinking.

Because I was not a driver at this point, I got dropped off back at home. I remember making it up to my room. By now, my oldest sister had moved out. So, I was sleeping in the top bunk bed, and my little sister slept in the lower bunk bed. The trundle was empty. I don't exactly know how I crawled up into that top bunk, but I somehow maneuvered my way up that bunk bed ladder and pulled myself into bed.

And then it began...

I lay my head back on that pillow and thought I was going to just go to sleep and have to deal with an upset stomach in the morning. That's what generally happens to me after having a few drinks. But that was not what was in store for me on that night.

You talk about body and soul!? As I lay on my back with my eyes closed, I began to feel my head just spinning! My head was not hurting. It was just spinning. I opened my eyes, thinking that would ease the spinning, but it did not.

I must not have remembered to turn off the light because the room was bright. I closed my eyes again, and that spinning intensified. "Oh, I think I drank too much!"

I could not move from that bed or from that position. After what seemed like an eternity, things changed, and not for the better!

Added to my head spinning, my body seemed to separate from my soul. I am not kidding; my soul seemed to say "I'm out of here!"

The next thing I knew, I felt my body on that bed, but I saw my soul floating up over me close to the ceiling. I am lying there on my back, and my soul is floating over me. It was like what you may have seen on

TV or in the movies. Think of Casper the Friendly Ghost flying in and out of places.

I was powerless to move or do anything but live in that disquieting moment. As my spirit floated, my head seemed to stop spinning. It was unreal. I can still remember how unreal it felt to be held down by something unknown and forced to experience this out-of-body moment.

At some point, I remembered praying, "Lord, please stop this thing," or simply moaning, "Oh my God!"

I must have had some of my faculties intact because I did not make any promises. You know, words that go something like "If you do this, I'll do that." Or "If you do this, I promise to never do that." It was as if I somehow knew a promise would be inappropriate. I just laid there watching. I have no idea when, but sometime during the night, my soul reunited with my body.

When I awoke the next morning, it was to the sound of my brother's voice saying, "Girl, you really drank last night; you could hardly get in bed; you are lucky Mom and Dad didn't hear you."

The light was streaming in from my bedroom window, and it scorched my eyes when I slowly fluttered my lashes toward the ceiling and tried to focus. The brightness was my signal that it was daytime, and I was one again.

"Yes, I did, and hopefully, I will not do that madness again!!" I tentatively responded as I scooted out of that top bunk and made my way past my brother to the bathroom, feeling happy that everything was moving together.

I was too inexperienced in my faith journey to know I needed to thank God immediately for working his miracle in my life that night. After that experience, I knew without a doubt what I needed. As a matter of fact, there is a song that came out in 1972. The group was called Soul Generation. They would smoothly croon the chorus – "Body and Soul. That's the way it's got to be."

Now, they may have been singing about finally being wed to the love of their life. But to me, it was recognizing that I needed my body and soul to remain as one. That period of temporal separation was not a happy place.

Now, please do not think that this was some complete turnaround, "I got this now" incident. No, I still went through the rest of college enjoying times when I drank with friends over a card game or when we went out dancing. Actually, it took me having children to decide I did not want to be a party drinker.

I did not want to have alcohol be the cause for any abnormalities during my pregnancies. After I began having children, it was easier not to drink because I just reminded myself that I only drank to have fun with my friends. The nine-plus months I carried my first child were filled with fun and laughter without alcohol. Since I never was one to drink by myself, I knew I would be fine.

I love the personal relationship I have with God. The spiritual moments I share in conversational prayer are priceless. I hope you can sense my elation that he is with me through my highs and lows. The most important lesson here is that I do know without a doubt that a united body and soul is the way it has to be!

Misunderstandings All Around!

Some 4th of July 2023 Thoughts on The Journey Towards Forgiveness
Luke 23:34 – Forgive them, for they know not what they do

The Fourth of July brings many things to mind. Folk like to cook out and have barbeques. They like to spend time with family. Shoot fireworks, some of which sound like army-weight canons being fired. One was so loud it knocked my security camera out of the window into a large potted plant. It made my husband and I jump up and simultaneously ask, "What was that!" and respond, "I don't know."

I heard a sermon yesterday where the minister reminded me that Fredrick Douglas once asked, "What to a slave is the Fourth of July?" It's a day that, more than any other day of the year, reminds him of all the gross misjudgments and cruelties that his people have become victims of.

The notion of celebrating a holiday that had no place in it for you as a Black person stuck with me and carried over to other thoughts about the July 4th holiday. Frederick Douglas must have felt that being asked to celebrate that holiday and asking him to encourage his people to celebrate was an indication that white America still misunderstood him and his people and what they desired.

Today, I have been thinking about all the times someone has said to me, "When are you coming back?" or "You should take the high ground." Or "I expect better of a reverend." "You are an educated woman. I expect you to handle this better." "Let it go." At my age, I had adhered to the "let it go" mantra too many times to count.

I can see the faces of those who have asked me to once again "let it go." In the past, each time, I would "let it go." And, because I had done so for so many years, it is surprising that it has been ten months, and I still have not returned. There has been a misunderstanding operating as truth. All around, I have been misunderstood.

Becoming aware of how I have misunderstood myself has caused me to consider how others have misunderstood me as well. So, after some moments of reflection, I began to pen what follows.

Forgiveness – what a powerful word. We think we can snap our fingers and forgive. Now, I am a faithful, spiritual child of God and believe I am saved by Jesus Christ, who shed His blood for our sins. God says to forgive as I have forgiven you (Matthew 6:14-15 says: For if you forgive other people when they sin against you, your heavenly Father will also forgive you. But if you do not forgive others their sins, your Father will not forgive your sins.).

I think we take the command lightly. Because when someone does something to us, we say I forgive you aloud. But do we really forgive? I genuinely believe we need God's grace. And thank goodness God is merciful and forgives us time and time again.

I began to ponder and said aloud, "I would like to propose the concept that there is forgiveness of the mind and forgiveness of the heart." Every once in a while, I begin acting as if I have something profound to offer. Anyway...

Let me try and work this thing out in my mind... Forgiveness of the mind is what we call on most of the time. Someone steals from you, and you forgive them. Someone kills someone you know or love, and you forgive them. Someone calls you names. Someone bullies you. Someone hits you. Someone ostracizes you. Someone tells lies about you.

Someone. Someone. Someone.

And you say I forgive you. And perhaps you do. But then they do it again... and then they do it again. And again!

And again!!

Scripture says Seven times seventy (Matthew 18:21-22 says Then Peter came to Jesus and asked, "Lord, how many times shall I forgive my brother or sister who sins against me? Up to seven times?" Jesus answered, "I tell you, not seven times, but seventy-seven times).

And one day, you say, I think I HAVE REACHED THAT SEVEN TIMES SEVENTY MARK. I can't do it anymore, and you walk away repeatedly, wondering, "Where is the doctor when you are standing in need of that spiritual miracle? Doctors can't help me. Neither Mom nor Dad can help me. My Christian friends can't help me. There is no more forgiveness here!"

Just how powerful is forgiveness of the mind?!

It's at this moment that I must turn to the only one who can make sense of this thing.

He is the only one who can manage this challenge of the mind. This hurt of the heart. It's at this moment that I have to seek a means to move from forgiveness of the mind to forgiveness of the heart.

I prayed that very moment and asked God, "What did it take for Jesus to pray, 'Forgive them for they know not what they do?'

God said to me that in my son's human body, His heart was pure. Jesus felt in His heart that they should be forgiven because they did not know what they were doing.

And at first, I did not get it. My mind told me, "But they did know." They said crucify him (Matthew 27:22-23). Judas turned him in after having eaten at the last supper (Mark 14:43-50). Peter knew he was denying him and felt ashamed (Luke 22:54-62).

Then, it became personal. Folk know what they have done to me. They do it over and over and over again. That's when God whispered so softly that my heart almost missed the Word. "You are forgiving with your mind and not your heart".

Then, with that sentence, He moved my heart so I could hear and understand.

"In my Son's heart, He knew that people did not know and do not know who He is. Perhaps people don't understand who you are."

And then I cried because His gentle words reminded my heart of who I am to Jesus. I felt such a strong love pouring into me at that moment. I felt loved.

There's nothing like those moments when God really allows me to feel His love. I know who I am because I know who Jesus is in me. Jesus is indeed the Son of God, the Son of Man, the Savior of us all; therefore, I give Him all the glory and praise. And truly, I know that I am a child of God, and Jesus loves me. And so, I, too, have to move to where I can honestly say, forgive them, Jesus, because they know not what they do.

Now, wait a minute because I am not there yet. But I am praying earnestly to get there. You see, I can forgive you in my mind. I can forgive and love you as my Christian brother and sister. But I am not where I should be.

I marvel at Jesus, our Savior, who can forgive us when we have been doing him injustices since the beginning of time. And He is still forgiving us. Not with a forgiveness of the mind. But with the complete loving forgiveness of the heart.

That's what I am striving for. If they knew who Jesus was, they would not have been able to hurt Him or His.

If we know who we are as children of God, how can we hurt one another repeatedly?

Wow! That is a gentle reminder that we also are guilty of hurting others. So, we who are guilty of hurting also have work to do.

Do you know who you are hurting? You cannot possibly know because if you did, you would stop the HURT!

As for me?

I am quickly moving to a place where I am going to ask for forgiveness, and I am going to forgive, not out of arrogance or self-righteousness, but with a humble, grateful heart. I am going to forgive just as God forgives me,

So, pray for me, and I will pray for you. You see, I am on a journey toward forgiveness of the heart because you cannot possibly know who I truly am. You can join me if you would like.

Yes, there were misunderstandings all around. I was misunderstood. I misunderstood myself. We all misunderstand what it means to forgive. If I think I have found the best response and end of this discussion, I misunderstand that, too. Yes, there were misunderstandings all around!!

HOSANAH TO THE KING WHO IS THE MASTER OF FORGIVENESS OF THE HEART!!

Sacrifice

A sacrifice I made for someone else or one someone made for me. That was the prompt in my senior citizen's creative writing class. Conversational French was another one of my classes this semester in 2022. Who knew that Wednesday's French class would give me an idea? I never thought I sacrificed anything in any significant way. I guess I believed sacrifice was a term reserved for major game players who made great strides for mankind. I don't fit in that category.

Anyway, our professor asked us to tell of a discovery we made about ourselves as a result of some event that occurred in our lives. Now, it is true that I have been blessed enough to learn and discover many things through the successes and failures in my life.

Now, in my French class we had to tell about this discovery in French. One thing I rediscovered was that in those five minutes, we had to come up with something to share, it is no easy task to converse in French well enough to share an event and then explain how it impacted my life. So, in a very elementary manner, I briefly shared my experience. In my best French-speaking-tones, I began...

Une grande découverte dans ma vie a été d'apprendre que je peux utiliser les choses de mon passé pour aider les autres aujourd'hui. Par exemple, je sais que le fait d'avoir été violée m'a aidé à atteindre d'autres jeunes femmes. Avoir eu un meilleur ami qui est gay m'a rendu vraiment compatissant et j'ai aidé les parents à éviter leurs enfants. Le fait d'être tombée enceinte à la suite d'un viol m'aide à comprendre celles qui pourraient avoir besoin d'avorter. Avoir des parents aimants a aidé à savoir comment être une mère aimante. Avoir Christ me rend fort. Quelle blessure m'a rendu fort.

You know, I have preserved the entirety of this short French piece within these paragraphs because I was so amazed that I was able to put these words together. My teacher and one other student actually understood what I was saying. Don't worry. I won't read the rest of it aloud.

I realize that paragraph may be difficult to translate from French to English. In summary, the self-learned message stated that "A big discovery in my life was learning that I can draw from my past to help others in my present." Let me explain in English.

When I was a junior in college, I was raped (even now, it takes me a minute to write that word because it invokes so many feelings in me and probably in others who read it. However, please remember that I was 20 years old then and over the years, I have traveled down many roads. Because I have written about that episode before, I will not go into the details here. Let's suffice it to say that with God and family, I long ago healed and moved to a healthy place.

But I did sacrifice my virginity on that day. I held such high ideals of saving myself for marriage. I believed what I had been taught in Sunday school. I held tight to that belief. I listened to what my parents said when they said wait.

Okay, I must admit that not having a single boyfriend up to that time kind of helped me in my effort to keep my virginity intact. However, it did not help me on that day. So, my dream was dashed in a few long, agonizing moments.

Something else I had been told in health classes and learned from my curious free time reading is that it was impossible to become pregnant after your first time. So, I had nothing to worry about, right?

As a result of those moments, I discovered I was pregnant.

I did all I could to push what happened out of my mind and go about my life. Well, my cycles were not reliable. One month, I would have one, and the next, I would not. My cycle would come when it felt like it and would last as long or short as it wanted. But I always had cramps.

Slowly I came to a place where I no longer thought about what happened to me. There were no red flags or sirens that went off. Then I noticed I just hadn't had a single cycle in three complete months.

Four months after the incident, while home from college for our six or seven weeks Christmas and winter break, I had to find a way to tell my parents what happened.

"You have to make a decision. You cannot have a baby and go back to school. Someone forced themselves on you." I could see that my Dad would like to have gotten his hands on the person who did it. Nevertheless, he and my Mom quickly moved to find a solution.

"I want to go back to school. And I have to have this baby because I do not believe in abortion."

"Do you want to marry this person?"

"No! I shouted. I just want to finish school and move on."

"Then you will have to give up the child."

So, I was torn. Another sacrifice. Loss of my virginity and now one of my Christians beliefs...

The process began. I was taken to a doctor who examined me. He called my parents into the room and told all of us together, "Yes, I can confirm that your daughter is pregnant. (Back in the day, the doctor talked to your parents about you. And, though they asked what I wanted to do, it was clear that the doctor looked to them because I was, for all intents and purposes, a minor).

"Here are her options. She can have this child. She can keep the child, or she can put it up for adoption. She can also abort the child."

"We have discussed this with Elizabeth, and she has decided to abort the child."

Hearing this said out loud made me very sad. But I kept silent, watched, and listened to plans being made for me.

The doctor continued. "I must let you know that she is about four months pregnant, and the procedure will not be the same as it would have been had she come to us earlier."

My parents and I looked puzzled. Of course, I had no knowledge about the process one way or the other. I guess my parents didn't either because they asked, "What will be involved?"

I remember his saying something like, "Because she is too far along, instead of coming to my office and having the procedure done here, she will have to be admitted into the hospital. She will be prepared for the abortion. However, she will go into labor and will go through delivery."

Now, this was a lot to take in. Just when you think you are grown and can handle it, all this happens.

I've lost my virginity. I have lost the ability to save myself for marriage. I have been helped to decide that I will not be able to have this baby, therefore losing the ability to tenaciously believe that abortion was wrong. And, now, I would not have my first child and the experience of basking in the newness of being a parent with my husband. Oh, but the jewel of the moment is that I would still give birth to my first child... only the child would be dead.

Oddly, I am trying to remember what I wore or whether it was snowing outside. I cannot recall what time it was when we left or whether the sun had already risen high in the sky. I do remember being at the hospital and being in that white half-wrap covering they put on you. I remember somebody sharing some words, telling me again about a process, and giving me my options. I remember my Mom and Dad being there mainly because they gave me a ride. I do not remember whether I was happy or sad. I was just numb and resigned to this decision.

Isn't it odd that I remember the experience of giving birth to my other three children in such vivid detail?

I know there was pain, and I remember seeing a big blob of blood. I remember the pressure of someone pushing on my stomach and being told I had to pass something called the afterbirth. It's like a haze. There were smells – I think... I remember catching a glimpse of them rushing away with that bloody blob or something. And then, I must have slept.

I am unsure how long I stayed in the hospital; maybe a day or two. I remember my parents explaining to my five siblings, "Elizabeth had to go to the hospital for a stomach virus." It would be a long time before they would know what actually happened.

The birth of my sacrificial lamb is such a blur.

However, I still have a picture of the sonogram of my lamb. It resurfaces every now and then when I look through old stored-away photos. Maybe someday my children will see the child growing in my womb captured in that milky-filmy, black and white, 4x4 inch photo and truly understand that they had an older sibling for just a little while that I felt and loved.

Sacrifices of a sort – for sure. Nevertheless, I believe we have these occurrences in our lives so that we can grow. But more importantly, so that we can, in turn, help someone else. Many times, I have been able to use my experience to help others.

I can share my story and empower others.

I am reminded that we are made stronger agents for good when we overcome obstacles. Sharing my experience with others is not the only way I can serve others. I also now can extend empathy and understanding to those who have had to endure this sort of intrusion. To be able to tell someone it is not your fault and truly know this to be true is a gift from God.

To say that you can get through this and soar and know it to be true is a gift from God. To say closure doesn't have to mean confronting, but it can be realized in using the power of the Holy Spirit to comfort and reach out. And that is truly a gift from God.

Today, I believe I did make some sacrifices.

A big discovery in my life was learning that I can draw from my past to help others in my present. In the grand scheme of things, perhaps I did not sacrifice that much. In my mediocre world, I thank God for seeing me safely through the sacrifice.

And maybe I did not know it then, but I surely know it to be true today. The experience has strengthened me. Avant Christ me rend fort. Quelle blessure m'a rendu fort. Translation: Having Christ makes me strong. What hurt me has made me strong.

Happy Places

The song just started filling my senses, and then I started swaying and moving to the counts – 1, 2, 3, 1, 2, 3. It was music from The Sound of Music. Do you know the song "My Favorite Things"? "Girls in white dresses with blue satin sashes, snowflakes that stay on my nose and eyelashes, these are a few of my favorite things." Her favorite things: "When the dog bites, when the bee stings, when I'm feeling sad, I simply remember my favorite things. Then I don't feel so bad."

I just kept playing that song over and over.

It is true though – I simply remember my favorite things, and then I don't feel so bad. My favorite things are my happy places. I have so many happy places that I retreat to whenever I wish. As I think about it, I could write a book about all my happy places!!

I smile as I remember one of my favorite things was dressing my girls, who are exactly 23 months apart in age. They actually have birthdays coming up in February 4 and January 4 of 2023.

I can see my little girls dressed in white dresses that belled out at the bottom. The dresses had blue, pink, or green sashes around the middle. My son, born September 11, would be dressed in a cute suit with shorts, a crisp shirt, a bow tie, and a little jacket or vest. Off we'd go to church.

Let me see... Learning and teaching make me happy. It seems like I have always been either learning or teaching something. One of my earliest memories is sitting on the steps of my home, reading a book. The funny thing is that I could not read. I remember my Mom smiling as she watched me. She would tell me later that I had the book turned upside down. But she knew I soon would have a deep love of books.

And I did. I could lose myself in books. Yes, I was one of those children who would have my head tucked up under a cover with a flashlight reading. I'd hear my Mom say, "Elizabeth, turn that light off and go to sleep." Or, I would be hanging upside down in a chair (you know, my legs would be propped up on the back of the chair, and my head would be dangling down towards the floor. I'd have a book in my hands reading away. "Elizabeth, you know you have nose bleeds. The blood is rushing to your head. Please get up from there and sit in the chair to read."

After school, I would go to the library and sit and read books or check some out to read at home. I could lose myself in the words as my eyes traced from page to page, image to image. I could find romance in the books. I could find adventure in the books. Nancy Drew. The Scarlet Letter. Langston Hughes and Tony Morrison. Reading is one of my favorite things! It is one of my happy places!

I taught school for about two and a half years. What a joy to see the smiles on the students' faces when they understood. At one point, I taught math to 5th and 6th graders who needed extra support. Their faces lit up when they understood they could learn tricks to remember portions of the timetable. One day, I realized they had difficulties with their 9 and 11 timetables...

"I want you to take a piece of paper and copy the two charts that I am going to draw on the board and listen as I explain them. Now raise your hand if you know how to count from 0 to 9 and 9 to 0."

They all raised their hands.

"Then, as long as you write 0 to 9 and then go back and write 9 to 0, you can say your 9 timetable", I said excitedly.

I drew the diagram on the board so they could visualize my words.

$9 \times 1 = 09$

$9 \times 2 = 18$

$9 \times 3 = 27$

$9 \times 4 = 36$

$9 \times 5 = 45$

$9 \times 6 = 54$

$9 \times 7 = 63$

$9 \times 8 = 72$

$9 \times 9 = 81$

9x10=90

As the light went on, understanding showed all over their faces. I said, "Now, let's do one more." Next, I drew the table for the 11's.

11x1= 11
11x2= 22
11x3= 33
11x4= 44
11x5= 55
11x6= 66
11x7= 77
11x8= 99
11x9= 99

"Okay now, notice that the numbers repeat themselves. Do you see the pattern, class?"

Heads bobbed up and down. Smiles were broad.

Take this home and look it over. We'll have a test on Friday. Everyone should be able to pass that test, right?"

"Yes", they shouted. When students get it, the teacher in me is in my happy place.

I went on to teach at the law firm where I worked. I would devise creative ways for those in my classes and on my team to use technology in many ways. I was happy when I saw their faces register that they grasped a concept or when they later would tell me they were using a technique I shared.

Law firms are document pushers. Attorneys make numerous changes: Move this paragraph. Change that numbering. Compare this section to that. Okay, now I need you to move that section over there, and please renumber the paragraphs. I need a Table of Contents. Can you now go back and do a Table of Authorities? By the time you have made what seems like and just might be the 100th rendition of a 200-page brief that has 500 numbered paragraphs and cited references on every other line, you may think you are done – but you are not.

You still need to create mailing labels for this brief that will be addressed to 100 different parties. You will need a means for automating these processes, not to mention the Excel spreadsheets and PowerPoint presentations that will be a part of the package.

It was my job to make this process less stressful by teaching best practices. Add problem-solving to my love of my daily teaching routine on a dily basis was a happy place for me.

You can only teach if you are willing to learn, right? I have been in one class or another all my life. Head Start, elementary, junior high, high school, a bachelor's degree, a master's degree, a doctor's degree, and Certificate programs.

I said to myself, "Liz, I have to laugh at the idea that you said you couldn't wait to finish that doctor's degree this past April, but you are now taking five SAGE classes. Yep, five, two, French classes, piano, stained glass, and creative writing. And you joined the Bowie Senior Center Chorale, where you are preparing for a Christmas Concert that includes singing in foreign languages.

Music and dance are a couple of my other happy places.

The music from The Sound of Music is still playing in the background. "Do, mi, mi. Mi, so, so. Re, Fa, Fa. La, ti, ti. When you know the notes to sing, you can sing almost anything!"

Music helps place me in the mood to put pen to paper.

I've been singing, dancing and playing the violin since I was a very young child. Music and dance are other places where I can be anyone I wish. If I want to dance in the trees and drink tea with jam and bread, I can do it. I can be one of the Sound of Music children, singing in a boat, or playing with the puppet show one moment and be off singing and tapping in the rain the next.

I thought the Hawaiian Wedding Song was so romantic that I sang it to my husband on our wedding day. It was our second time being married. He stood at the altar, waiting for me to come down the aisle.

I was definitely in my happy place. But you know someone will try to make you sad when you are happy.

No one knew I would sing except my brother, who played the song for me. I did not sing it during the wedding rehearsal, and it was not put on the printed program. Anyway, someone who would need the wireless microphone later in the service would not give it to my son to bring to me. So, I turned to an usher and asked, "Would you please go and get the microphone because we cannot begin until I have it."

I saw the usher say something, and a few minutes later, the microphone was brought to me. I was able to go back to my happy place. The doors opened, and my handsome husband stood in his black tailored tuxedo, crisp white shirt, stunningly sharp red bowtie, cummerbund, and pocket square.

My oldest brother who was dressed similarly to my husband, took my arm and led me just inside the door. And I began "This is the moment. I've waited for..." A Happy Place!

But my happiest place...?

I CELEBRATED MY 63RD birthday on Sunday, November 27th. I shared the day with my husband, and my children and grandchildren who live in this area (my middle daughter and her family moved to Spokane, Washington). I had hinted to my son, daughter, and husband that I wanted to host a Christmas tree-decorating brunch. Because it was my birthday, I didn't want to cook. So, I ordered breakfast and lunch food from Bob Evans. I also ordered vegan options for my son from Silver Dollar.

A little past noon, I heard the doorbell being rung repeatedly. "That's Kyrie, isn't it?"

My son, Langford, said, "You know it is."

As he opened the door, I noticed the sky was still slightly overcast, and the air was brisk. Four grandkids came through the door and, one at a time, greeted me with a hearty "Hello, grandma" and a wonderful hug.

My oldest, Lauren, came next and greeted me with a "Happy Birthday!"

They quickly took off their coats, and those who preferred to go barefoot shed their shoes and made ready for our day.

"Come everyone, let's gather around for prayer. So, we can eat." Everyone moved around the dining room table, and I asked, "Okay, who would like to pray?"

Kalvin said, "I'll do it."

"Kalvin, you'll do it?" I confirmed.

"Yes, I'll do it. Let us pray. Dear Lord, thanks for this day when we can gather together. Thank you for our family. I pray that we will have a great day. Thank you for the food that has been prepared. It is in Jesus' name that we pray. Amen."

"Amen!"

"Thank you, Kalvin. Okay, let's eat."

I put on a playlist, and we dined to the sounds of soulful Christmas music. After breakfast, we began to make Christmas ornaments. I showed them how to take Styrofoam balls and how to use small clear push pins to attach bright red, silver, gold, and green sequins to the ball. A red ribbon was attached so the ornaments could be hung the tree. We chatted and laughed and had so much fun. While some of us continued to work on the ornaments, others brought up the Christmas tree and other ornaments from the basement.

"Hey, there are some clear bulbs over there that will need to be hung on the tree as well. I like to add something else new each year; it brings newness to the season," I said.

"Okay," the kids said as they began opening the boxes.

"We can also add the ceramic houses to the angels and other things in the window. They are in that crate over there," I continued. "Raggedy Ann and Andy can be placed on that wooden ledge. Skip, can you take the backs off so we can put the batteries in them."

He put in the batteries, and then, over our soulful Christmas music, I heard Raggedy Ann and Andy start to sing as they did their dance.

Their dancing seemed to tickle my husband as he chuckled in his deep voice. "They are something else." He laughed.

As the kids grew hungry, they would return to the table and grab something else to eat and drink. So, in between eating, we all decorated that 7-foot tree with nice and full branches. No Charlie Brown tree for me.

"What about these present boxes?" asked Skip.

"Do they open?" asked Kyrie.

"No, they light up." Said Langford. "Put one set on either side of the fireplace."

Three red, green, and blue mesh boxes with bows were unstacked and put on either side of the fireplace. The light flowing from them added a nice glow to the room when they were plugged in.

Okay, the last thing we need to do is add the decorations we made to the tree." Off they scooted to bring their decorations and place them on the tree.

"Turn off all the other lights so we can see what we have created here." That was Skip's suggestion. We agreed, and off went the lights. We smiled and nodded as we admired our work and basked in the warm spirit of Christmas that had begun to fill the house on that day in November.

It was my birthday, and I had been ushered into the start of my happiest place of each and every year. It is Christmas Season, and I have 27 days to be in my happy place, anticipating the celebration of the birth of Christ.

Those Unanswered Prayers

Times like today, when prices are rising, and the electric, gas, and water bills are skyrocketing, I reminisce about the past as I live my present. I'm in the backroom of our basement, reaching up to hang freshly washed clothes on the indoor clothesline. I think back over the years and remember wanting to have a dryer because I did not want to have to hang clothes like I did when I was a young girl.

We did not have a dryer, so, yes, we hung our clothes on lines in the backyard. Not only that, but we also did not have a dishwasher for many years, so we took turns washing the dishes our family of eight would use during meals. Paper plates were for picnics.

Here in our Fort Washington Home, there is no dishwasher. In our Waldorf, there is one, but we hardly ever used it when my children were small, and it never gets used now. It isn't even plugged in.

We did not even have a vacuum cleaner as a child, so we swept the floors. For many years, there were no carpets. No high-shine floor polish that went on in one coat. My dad and brothers stripped, scrubbed, polished, and buffed all those hardwood floors.

My daughter, who is also my middle child, asks what or why things are as they are and why she does this or that. Who is she like? Each time she came to me with a "Did I" question, I took her seriously and did all I could to help her trace that moment back to its origins as I remembered it. So, while hanging the clothes, I also began to make a mental list of the sayings, and rules that I grew up with that still impact my life today.

On Sundays, all eight of us (Mom, Dad, three girls, and three boys) went to church, period.

Take someone's hand when you cross the street.

At seven, when I burned my stomach while fixing my little brother's formula, I learned that my Mom and Dad would always look after me.

Don't climb on things so much – I broke my toe, ignoring that one.

Be careful playing with those boys. My glasses were broken when a pitched hardball hit me in the face.

Stay in the yard – I was constantly climbing the fence.

Don't put your elbows on the table. Say, thank you.

Let others see your talent – They would ask us to perform for the company.

Change your underwear. You may have to go to the doctor.

Come let me fix your hair – pressing hair can be pretty uncomfortable. The other type of kitchen was the hair at the nape of my neck.

Music makes the chores easier to bear. In our home, the air was always full of music, singing, and dancing.

Don't make her nose bleed – I had frequent nose bleeds, and my siblings were under strict orders not to make it bleed or face the consequences.

Defend one another – no one was allowed to mess with my younger siblings.

Eat your vegetables. I still don't like them, but my children always willingly ate them.

Let's watch TV together and play board games together.

We take vacations together.

You look like your dad.

My parents are pretty cool.

Sacrifice for your children – my parents always did.

Sometimes you have to do things you just don't understand — wear ugly glasses, old lady shoes, not have a lot of clothes, no shoes with heels, no stockings, no nail polish, no lipstick,

Come in the house before dark.

Cross the street at the corner.

Behave yourself when you are in the street because you never know who knows your parents and will tell on you. We went to lunch with friends. We paid for our meal, but some of those who were with us didn't. Someone at the 5-and-dime saw us and told my Mom.

Get good grades in school. If I got a "C," I was the one who heard you can do better than this. – I rebelled for a moment in college and didn't care. But now, I just can't deal with bad grades – even when I'm auditing the course.

One of the most important things my parents told me at a very young age was, "Be patient. Your turn will come." A very real concern when you are one of six children. I would hear it over and over again. I realize the benefits of being patient now. But, sometimes, it sure was hard back then.

I had to wait to go to school because I turned five after the cut-off date for entering kindergarten. I had to wait to wear cool shoes because something was said to be wrong with my feet.

I had to be patient and just wear those cat eyeglasses. I had to be patient in kindergarten, because I would have friends someday. I had to be patient and understand that I would not always be called ugly. I had to be patient when I wanted to wear pants to school. I had to be patient with having a birthday so close to Thanksgiving that I could get a little lost in the holiday festivities. I had to be patient and allow life to run its course. This is a lot for a little girl who hadn't even turned eight yet.

This notion of being patient and waiting your turn began when I was a little girl, but it has played a major role in my ever-continuing development.

Garth Brooks sings "Unanswered Prayers." And I totally get it now.

If not for being patient and waiting my turn, I would have passed up the opportunity to meet my first boyfriend, who married me twice. I had to be patient and wait to find a husband to and give birth to our three beautiful children because I thought I would never have a family. Now I even have eight grandchildren!

Back in kindergarten, I thought I would never have friends to play with at school. However, being patient was rewarded by the many good friends I have met throughout my life.

The glasses thing went full circle. I didn't like them and didn't want to wear them because others said they made me ugly. Well, I wore contacts for a while. However, I now wear my glasses and am quite comfortable in them. Patience. I had to have patience.

There were so many talented people in my high school, where I majored in music. There were so many talented people in each place I took dancing. So, I had to be patient until my turn came to excel in the arts. Be Patient, Liz!! I was self-published once and published by others twice. I am still waiting for my doctor's dissertation to be published.

I am learning to be patient. I think...

You know, I really prayed for the things I wanted. Let's call it prayer because I would often be alone in my room, just crying to someone, talking silently, and making my needs known. I prayed to get rid of those glasses. I prayed to have friends. I prayed to have a boyfriend. I wondered why I couldn't go to school with other five-year-olds.

But thank God for unanswered prayers. I look at who I am becoming and what I have in my life, and I know that if some of my prayers had been answered, I wouldn't be here. My Mom and Dad would say to be patient. Your turn will come. And it does just that.

Garth Brooks sang about the love of his life. Again, I can identify. Suppose God had answered the times I had a crush on someone or thought someone was the one. So many things would be different. So, I have deep love and appreciation for my children and grandchildren, and my husband for continuing to want to love me as hard as they can.

Garth Brooks, I, too, have to thank God for some of those unanswered prayers!

Improv During Acting Class

Another Day's Journey

With all the violence and abuse that we hear about all over the news, in movies, and on sitcoms, it seems like we can't get away from this thing. We as parents never stop fearing that something will happen to our children. So, this piece is written to keep us vigilantly caring for our children – no matter what.

The assignment was to conjure up a scene in our minds and to play that scene only by emotions that pass across our faces. We were not to say a word, only think of the scene. But our faces should show a myriad of emotions. In the moment, this is the scene that came to my mind to use as an emotional trigger.

The woman wakes up from a disturbing dream that recurs occasionally. Screaming and unnerved, a shadow of who she is. Is it possible that the dream is true?

She goes into her morning routine. She stretches and sings, "It's Another Day's Journey." As she goes through the dressing process, shadows emerge in her visage. Emotions run the gamut as she voices the content of her dream aloud. Does it stem from some long-ago past event that has been pushed to the recesses of her mind? It seems to grow larger and larger each time. Trying to take over her peace of mind.

This distraught woman sees her little infant brother, who is 7 years younger than her, seems to be sleeping on the couch, and a shadow gets on top of that tiny baby and begins to rub against him.

The shadow comes into view, and it's her. Is that possible? Could she have done this thing? He was a baby. She was a child. Would she have had those feelings at seven years old? She again slips into that dark place where she doesn't know what to do.

Over and over again, the dream comes.

She is now 75 years old. She suddenly yells, "Oh Lord, have mercy on my soul!!" She then begins to pull herself together and continue her morning ritual as she sings, "It's Another Day's Journey." she unzips the bag, puts on the clergy robe, picks up the bible, and moves to the church. "Today's sermon is about..."

I allowed the emotions to fade from my face as I lowered my head in a final movement as the scene I conjured up for a class fades to black and say another silent prayer asking God to protect my children and grandchildren. Lord protect the children of this world.

Fake It Until You Make It

The month is October, and the year is 2022. I sit here smiling and thinking about the lengths I used to go to be accepted. Who did I think I was fooling? For so long, eyeglasses were the bane of my existence. But there was a point when things were fine. The days when I never really paid much attention to the way I looked.

In my child's mind, life was about playing with family and friends, dreaming about the future, and being happy. I skipped and laughed often, did summersaults, and skinned my knees. I was not really afraid of new things and meeting new people. My mother and father made us feel safe. But it is incredible how life can turn your innocent or naïve laughter into a cautious, protective attitude of angst.

The first time I knew I needed help was when my teacher told my parents I was squinting in class and seemed to have difficulty seeing what was on the blackboard. I had been faking it, but my teacher was right; I could not see that board. My parents took me to the eye doctor, who said I needed glasses. I was okay with that until those "wonderful" little people at school made fun of them. Suddenly, I realized that perhaps this glass thing was a mistake.

"Why did I have to wear those things? How could I live in my world wearing those things and waiting for the next time I'd be called monk, four eyes, or ugly?" Oh, I had to devise a way to fake it until I could make it. This thing with the eyeglasses was getting worse and worse. Oh, don't think, for a second, I hadn't tried to take steps to fix this dilemma.

First, I picked out some nice fashionable frames the next time I went to the optometrist.

I picked out some stylish octagon-shaped wireframes I had seen some actresses wearing on TV. "I want those!" I exclaimed.

The doctor replied, "I'm sorry, Elizabeth, but your prescription will make your lens too heavy for that frame to hold." I was crushed.

The doctor turned to my parents and suggested, "Mom and Dad, I can show you some frames that will hold Elizabeth's lens, and we can make her lens thinner, but it will cost more."

Then I heard that oft-repeated, mood-altering parental reply, "We can't afford the extra money."

I knew this was true because we were a family of eight, and it was hard enough to make ends meet. This did not keep me from being disappointed, though.

I was allowed to pick a frame that the doctor said would minimize the thickness of the lens.

When I got those cat-shaped framed eyeglasses, the lens hung over the sides of the frames by about half an inch. I hung my head, put them on, and said, "Oh well – can't fake it this time."

Then I thought I had an answer when I heard about this thing called contact lenses. Wow, I just put these little circles in my eyes, and I would not have to wear any glasses. My wish would be granted. No more glasses!! Imagine my joy at the thought that the next time I had to go to the eye doctor, I would be able to get contact lenses.

Full of anticipation and excitement, I headed with my parents to get my new glasses. I went through the usual exam where I could barely read the tremendous, big E at the top of the chart. I had read that chart so many times that I remembered it, and yes, I did fake that because I just said what I could remember. When I couldn't remember anymore, I just guessed. Okay, so I could fake it to the second line of the chart.

I just couldn't see.

TO BE CONTINUED...

My Long-Termer

I have never been able to get away. It has been a long time since we began this love-hate, on-again-off-again affair. It has made me laugh, cry, smile, and frown... I have had this relationship since I was six or seven. My longest-lasting relationship.

No, I mean it. Nothing in my life has had such a continuous impact. From our introduction, it has never ceased to make itself known.

We change in our relationships. Our looks change. Our bodies change. Sometimes, our coloring changes. Change, but the relationship endures.

I was a regular kid, going about my own business, thinking I was doing okay. Then I went to school. We were not introduced at my first school. Born in November, I went to Headstart before kindergarten. That's where kids who turned five after the October 31st deadline began their education.

We played so much in Headstart and did not read to ourselves, so and I was unaware that I needed my long-termer remained hidden.

In elementary school, a teacher noticed I squinted and didn't see the writing on the blackboard. After she conversed with my Mom and Dad, it was decided that I needed a doctor to examine my eyes.

"Okay, this sounds like a nice adventure. I'm going to get something new."

Off we went to have my eyes checked. The office was bright and clean. I got in that great big chair – big for a little girl.

Looking around at everything, it crossed my mind, and I said, "Good, I don't see anything that looks like a needle in this place." That was important to me, then. Actually, it is important to me now, too.

The doctor did an eye exam. I could see that great big black E on the eye chart. But then the doctor started going down the chart. (I have that thing memorized now. One doctor's voice now sounds like the next.)

"Read the next line," The doctor directed.

"F," "P". "I have this," I said to myself. "I can see those letters on that chart all the way across that room." It actually was only a short distance away.

Then he did it. He went down two lines. "I can't see that," I murmured.

He then put me in a chair, put different lenses in a machine that he turned this way and that, and asked, "Is that better or worse? I responded in kind.

We did that back and forth a few times, and then he was ready to tell my parents what he thought. It was determined that I would get glasses.

Next, we went and checked out eyeglass frames. Eagerly, I looked at the ones I liked. Mom, I want that one.

They checked the price – "That's out of our price range."

"What price range are you looking for?" After that, the eye doctor showed us the frames in our price range.

Then, I picked out some octagon-thin eyeglass frames. I still felt delighted seeing them because I had seen Goldie Hawn on Laugh-in wearing some. They were really great looking. "I would like those!"

Then, a disappointing voice said, "Your lenses will be too heavy for those." Even a six- or seven-year-old can feel frustrated.

"Let me show you what will work best for your frames."

I thought, "That crazy person is showing me some little cat-eye glasses."

No, really, they were shaped like a cat's eyes. The rim was black instead of the cool wire of those granny glasses. You know, Granny on the Beverly Hill Billies wore the ones I liked, too. I looked to my parents for support. They supported me by saying, "Yes, well, we'll take those then."

"Really?" They had selected those cat glasses. Oh well, at least they let me pick out a blue frame.

The relationship was about to begin.

It took two weeks to make the eyeglasses. When they were ready, we headed back to pick them up. I believed I knew what to expect. I did not like that frame, but I could handle it.

"Elizabeth Ellis?" I heard my name, looked at my Mom, and waited for her to get up and take me back to get my glasses. I sat in the chair, excited to get my new glasses. They pulled out a pair of glasses. They were blue, all right. But then I became confused.

"What are those things?" Of course, I said this to myself. "This can't be right!" They had the thickest lenses I had ever seen in my life. Those lenses had to be two inches thick, hanging over the frames' sides so anyone could see the thickness. Do you know how thick the bottom of a Coke bottle used to be when it was made of glass? That's what those lenses looked like.

"Let's try them on," the eyeglass lady said.

I frowned. I did not want to put those things on. I followed instructions and put them on.

"Take a look."

Man, those things made me look crazy. Yes, even at that age, I knew when I looked crazy. The lenses were so thick that the blue cat frames seemed lost. They were so thick that they made my eyeballs look very small. It was the first, but not the last, time I would feel I wasn't very pretty in my long-termers.

My parents paid the money, and off I went with those things on my eyes because they said I had to wear them all the time. I could see better with the glasses on, but I'm not sure it was worth it.

That was the beginning of our relationship. From that time on, it would be putting glasses on and taking them off. "I hated those things. Why am I wearing them? Mom, can't I wear contact lenses?" I would beg.

On and on it would go:

"The doctor said your sight is too bad, and you cannot wear them. Plus, they are too expensive."

"Can I try that eyeglass frame?"

"Your prescription is too high."

"Can I get thinner lenses?"

"We can't afford them."

By the time I got to high school, I was tired of being called names, coke bottle, four eyes, monk, seeing the looks, hearing the bad news that I wasn't a candidate for this or that, and believing the hype – until I decided I would wear those glasses when I had to.

So, in college, I walked around half-blind because I would only wear them when I had to read something.

Friends would wave at me and wonder why I was frowning. "Are you mad or something?"

"Nope," I'd say. "I just couldn't see you."

Then it became the norm for folk to say, "Elizabeth or Liz, stop frowning and put your glasses on."

When I went to live in New York at 22, almost 23, I decided to get some contact lenses. I did, and life was much better. I didn't have to wear those awful glasses. But I still had to wear lenses, and back then, they were expensive. But the cost was worth it to me. I did all I could not to have to wear glasses.

I was always told I was not a candidate for that Lasik procedure. But then, in my late forties or early fifties, it was discovered that I could benefit from the procedure, and I eagerly had it done.

"Wow, now I don't need to wear any glasses or contact lenses. I can see. Look at that. I can see. Wow, this lifelong relationship with those glasses is finally over!"

Perhaps not...

Yes, today, I really do not have to wear glasses anymore unless I am reading something small. Also, today, the lenses on reader glasses do not have to be Coke-bottle thick. My readers can be as fashionable as anyone else's glasses. So, wearing them when necessary is not a big deal anymore.

Then, life began catching up with me again. Now, I am at a place where my relationship with my long-term partner has changed from annoying despair to respect and gratitude. Why, you ask?

Because my vanity has reared its unpredictable, unrealistic head, I'm getting older, and I do not wear makeup to dim the lines forming on my forehead like my dad's or the telltale puffiness under my eyes. As long as I am not frowning, the frown lines still are not visible.

Thankfully, my long-termer hides the puffiness of aging and actually makes me look a little less like I am 63 and more like a pretty cool lady for an old woman. Probably not much difference, but I wear my glasses all the time now, even though I don't need them.

Times flies by and my need for my longer termer changes. At first I would have to roll over, in the morning, and pick up my glasses before putting my feet on the floor, because my eyesight could be compared to what you see when you drive in a torrential downpour. Then I was would roll over and put my glasses only because they make me feel better about the way I look.

I am 63 years old. Fifty-seven years, and we're still going strong!

My long-termer is something else, isn't it? Or is it?

Tales of New York?

Just about everyone who dreams of being in the arts also has a dream of living in New York City ("NYC"). In 1982, at the ripe old age of 22, my dreams of becoming a dancer were running wild.

Having graduated from college, I returned home from Ohio to Washington, D.C., and landed a summer job at the U.S. Department of State. It seemed as though my dreams of being a dancer would be put on hold as I headed towards a career as a State Department overseas officer.

While working that summer, I discovered that I could apply for a position at the State Department office in NYC. So, I began to come up with a plan about how I could work at State and dance as well. I submitted the paperwork to transfer and began searching for a place to live in NYC.

As I reflect on it, I never considered how this might make my parents feel, seeing as I had just returned from Ohio. I should not have been surprised when they said, "We don't want you to move to New York. You are too young and don't have immediate family there."

"But I want to dance. I really want to dance." I responded. "I can do this."

"I'll drive you." My Dad finally conceded.

My State Department transfer was approved, and I had one month to find a place to live and get settled in. The plan was to search for a hotel or a place where I could live until I could find an apartment. It all seemed so easy – at least it did in my mind. I started looking up hotels and located some in Manhattan that were in my price range. After several rounds of searching, I finally found one, and sight unseen, I made a reservation.

I had been to NYC many times with my parents as a child. Also, I visited with friends during college breaks. So, of course, I was prepared for the big city move. I could see it clearly. A smile began to form on my face as things appeared to be going well and I would soon be on my way. I had that star wanna-be mindset. I only saw the glitter and glamour of my big break possibilities. So, if the place I found was in the heart of the city, I figured that was further confirmation that I could do this thing.

We packed up the car with my belongings. I said my goodbyes to my Mom and those siblings who were around, and off my Dad and I went to get me started on this exciting new adventure.

What was there not to be excited about? I had a job and a place to live. I had money saved for my dwelling. I would be close to where I would go to realize my dream of becoming a dancer. Did I forget to mention that I had set my sights on dancing at Alvin Ailey? And

That morning, we rolled down our Southeast Washington, D.C. street. Both sides of our street were lined with semi-detached houses. Some were bordered by hedges and others by fences, and each boasted small green lawns and flower gardens.

"I'm on my way," I said as I did my internal happy dance. I prepared for the five-hour drive and looked out the windows to take in everything I would see on the way.

Did I mention how excited I was? Yes indeed! We were barely on the Baltimore-Washington Parkway heading north before I dozed off to that semi-conscious place where I could dream and still hear everything around me.

I only came fully awake at the gas station and restroom stops. The next fully conscious moment I remembered was entering the tunnel, signifying our arrival in New York. Everything was right on schedule. I had the day to get my things in the room and spend some time with my Dad before he left. Then I would get my bearings about the area and make plans for starting work on Monday.

As my Dad drove along, I swiftly turned my head right and left, looking for the address of the place I would call my temporary home. As we continued driving into the city, I began to notice things.

"Hum, this isn't very clean. But that's okay. I'm sure where I'm staying will be fine."

I glanced at my Dad from the corner of my eye and noticed the crinkles beginning to form on his brow. He said nothing, but I could tell he wasn't pleased. I did not say anything, either. I was determined to see this through. After all, I did want to dance.

Dodging our way through the crowded streets towards our destination, emotions seemed to be about to burst. We both were silently wondering what the outcome of this journey would be. Although I was not feeling defeated, I was concerned. Not that I wouldn't be okay, but that my Dad might not leave me there.

Man, why couldn't this first day be like that day long ago when my Mom and Dad had brought the six of us here for a vacation? I still remember peering into the NBC television station window watching the Today show. Maybe it seemed so fantasy-like because I spent a lot of time looking up at the tall buildings and being in awe at being in the city I had seen on T.V. Back then, things just seemed tall and awesome.

Well, we pulled up in front of a place that did not resemble any hotels I had stayed in before. By now, the sun had begun to set, and things looked even grimmer. Folks were coming in and out of the place. But more importantly, there were these women who stood around outside.

I'm sure my eyes looked larger to those who saw them through my eyeglasses. My hopeful demeanor began to shift as it all began to sink in. I knew those females were not Broadway actors, restaurant waitresses, or hotel helpers. I looked out the window, then back to where my belongings were stowed in the car.

I didn't dare look at my Dad. I put one hand on the door handle, thinking, "Let me hurry and get out and make a run for it. I did not know how I was going to get all my stuff out of this car though."

I must have been imagining that I was a magician or Olympic sprinter. Or I must have thought I was superwoman who could leap tall buildings, because in my young, crazy mind, I thought that I could make this mad dash before my Dad uttered a single word. I thought my insane plan had a chance until one of those women approached the car and peeked in the window.

Ridiculous excitement turned to heartbroken resignation. I still hadn't looked at my Dad, but I lowered my hand from the handle and sat back in the seat.

I finally looked over at him, and he was lowering his brow, wrinkled gaze from the window to look at me. He said four words before he started the car back up. "You can't stay here."

I knew he did not mean only at this hotel. He meant not in NYC.

New York Part II

Needless to say, the ride home was quietly pensive, and the air was pregnant with my disappointment. The five-hour drive now seemed like it took 10 hours. New York faded in the background as New Jersey came into sight.

I cannot even remember what played on the radio as we made our way through Pennsylvania, a small portion of Delaware, and then through Maryland. I drifted in and out of sleep as I considered my predicament. I still had not figured out what to do when we pulled up in front of our home, unpacked the car, and went back into the house. I went up the stairs to the room I shared with my little sister.

Oh well, I would have to be content with being back home for the night. I'm sure my parents were happy I was safe.

Maybe a day later, I called the New York State Department Office. "Hello, I couldn't find a place to live in New York. So, I need more time. Can you hold my position while I search for a place?" I asked.

The voice on the other end of the line stated, "We can hold your position for two more weeks. After that, the offer will be rescinded." Then, all I heard was silence.

"Thank you for the additional time," I said in my glass-half-full voice.

Unfortunately, those two weeks came and went, and I still could not find a place to live. The job offer was rescinded, and I thought I would have to give up on that dream.

Not only that, when my transfer was approved, I gave up the position in the D.C. State Department Office. So, I would have to look for another job as well.

I STILL LOVED NEW YORK. So, I found my way back to New York and ended up looking around Brooklyn College. I was considering applying to the college to get a degree in Dance.

I passed by a message board and saw an apartment for rent notice on an 8½ sheet of paper – the kind of notice with a line drawn to separate the information from the phone numbers that I could tear off. After pulling off one of the tags, I went to find a phone booth to place a call.

When a man answered the phone, I said, "I pulled your number off of an apartment for rent ad at Brooklyn College. Is it still available?"

"Yes, it is," the man said.

"I'm interested in renting it," I replied.

"It's a one-year lease, and you must have the first and last months' rent up front."

"Can I see the place?"

"Sure."

We set a time that day, and I went to see the place. It was located right across the street from Brooklyn College.

Brooklyn was a multicultural and multi-ethnic place. On one side, where the apartment was located, were homes primarily occupied by Jewish people. Not far down the street, African Americans, Jamaicans, and other people of color lived.

I believe the apartment was on the second or third floor. There was no elevator, but I don't remember it being a problem getting up to the place.

But that could have been because I had been dancing and was in pretty good shape in my twenties.

Anyway, I was still hopeful because the apartment was far enough out of the busy section of Brooklyn but near enough for me to catch a subway into Manhattan. The man was there to show me the place. In a kind voice, he said, "There is a living room and dining combination; the small kitchen is here. There is a stove and oven, a refrigerator, and cabinets. But the oven on the stove does not work."

"The oven doesn't work?" I repeated. "That may be okay," I said pensively.

"The bedroom is pretty large and has a nice-sized bathroom." I followed him into the bathroom and nodded that it was satisfactory.

"Okay, I have to let you know that the ceiling in the bedroom needs to be repaired," He hurriedly began. I looked up at the ceiling and saw a big gaping hole.

The look on my face must have said a lot because he quickly continued, "But I will get that done right away. And I'm willing to take a hundred off the first month's rent."

Well, that would help me out, I thought. I will now need $900 for the first month's rent and the security deposit to move in. He did say he would fix the ceiling. So, my hopes began to rise again. The floors were hardwood, and they at least had a beautiful sheen. This apartment had plenty of room for me.

"If you want it, you can move in at the first of the month."

"I think that will work, and I look forward to moving in at the first of the month!"

So, my plans were set again. I had enough money saved for the rent and enough to carry me for a little while. So, I headed back home to D.C. to ask my parents to take me back to New York again.

The only thing was I still did not have a job...

End Of Part Two
A Brief Look Into My Dad

My Dad is such a large part of the preceding memory, I thought it would be nice to share a brief glimpse of the man I call Dad.

–It's impossible to capture the lifetime of experiences I shared with my Dad in a few words. He taught me what I needed to know about how I should be treated as a girl and a woman. We would chat about whatever was going on in the world. I learned from the great example he lived. You know – his actions, time, and commitment were extremely valuable. I believe my siblings felt the truth in this statement: I think my Dad made each of us feel special and unique while, at the same time, he and Mom believed in keeping us united as a family.

Being a World War II veteran didn't affect his ability to function in civilian life. He was a caring, strong, no-nonsense man. We knew that though there were six of us, he wanted each and every one of us. His mother died when he was about 3 months old, and his father was confined to a mental hospital and passed when he was young. He had one brother that he never knew because it is thought that he passed early as well. So, being an only child, he wanted to have a large family. That is right. My parents had six children.

When my parents were having children, having an abortion was not the norm, and my Mom told me she was not the type who would consider the back-alley abortion that some opted for back then. Birth control did not seem to be an option either.

Anyway, he spent lots of time with us. My Dad took us on long walks. We would smile and laugh at his crazy jokes. He played board games with us. We went to church together, whether we had a car or had to walk. He would walk to work when that was the only mode of transportation available. He cooked and cleaned. He ran alongside my bike until I could ride it upright and not bend the training wheels.

He played sports with us, and I eagerly watched baseball with him. He would go to my dance recitals and graduations. I would go with him to visit our relatives on his side of the family. I would hang out with him at Bethlehem Baptist Church, where he was a trustee and a deacon. He also printed items for the church using an old-fashioned mimeograph machine, and he was the church custodian.

Many say that if there had been more acceptance of Negroes when he was younger, he would have played professional baseball. He was a member of the Negro Baseball Team, the Knights, and we still have the jersey he wore.

I think he was about 5 feet 7 inches. He was never overweight, and he was in good shape. He was the type who could eat raw eggs, and he could eat tomatoes as if they were apples.

Meals needed to have three parts – vegetable, starch, and meat.

On holidays, he never missed an opportunity to show how much he cared about my Mom. He may not have showered her with expensive gifts, but my Mom said he picked out cards with the most beautiful words.

Their love was not full of hugs and kisses all over the place. It was just fun and real and sincere.

Nevertheless, towards the end, he was very frail, and his illness and loss of awareness showed on his face and in his frame. Oh, how I thank God that I mainly have memories of that strong, handsome, caramel-colored, light brown-eyed man who was the spitting image of his dad down to the premature graying of his hair.

He left us too soon. I was pregnant with my youngest, my son, when he passed. He's been dead more than 30 years, and can you believe I can still see his smiling face and hear his hearty chuckle? He died from complications due to Alzheimer's and Diabetes.

That's just a snapshot of the man who was my loving father.

Was My Mom Really Happy When I Was Born

Was my Mom really happy when I was born,? My oldest grandchild asked.

I took my eyes off the road for a couple of seconds and quickly glanced at the look on her face. She was peering at me earnestly, waiting for me to respond. I determined she was serious even though I was slightly surprised by her question.

"Your mother," I chuckled softly. "Yes, as the saying goes, she was 'over the moon'. She was so happy that you were here. I was very happy too.

"Was my Dad happy?" She continued.

"Yes. Your Dad was happy, too. Everyone was happy. I was ecstatic. I was there when you first poked your head into this world. It was a wonderful time for all of us. You were your Grandpop and my first grandchild.

"Everyone was happy". I chuckled at the memory, "By the way, I was in the room when all eight of my grandchildren were born."

"Oh." She said as she made me the beneficiary of a rare small smile that turned up the sides of her mouth just a bit.

That brief time of sharing seemed to please her, and she returned to listening to her music as we rode along in silence. The country music that was playing on the car radio faded into the background as my mind returned to that day almost 18 years ago...

We were in the delivery room, and my daughter was on that whiter-than-white bed, waiting for things to get going. It was her first child. Even with her belly protruding, she still looked tiny in that bed. She was quiet. To the nurses and other medical team in the room, she probably looked strong and as if she did not have a care in the world.

To her mother, who had been down that road, she looked like my firstborn daughter who was about to be welcomed into one of the best parts of womanhood—becoming a mother. I smiled to myself at the possibilities that awaited her.

Then a contraction hit, and from where I sat at the side of her bed near her head, I rubbed her arm, smiled, and nodded. My daughter did not utter a sound, and very little expression passed across her face. So, it was barely noticeable that the pain had ripped through her abdomen. Ever so slightly, she grimaced, and just as quickly, her face returned to normal, and she gazed ahead.

I knew it would not be long before another contraction would rear its nerve-racking head. We chatted about this and that and nothing at all as we waited for the next time...

And it came again, and the pressure on my hand deepened a little more. However, she still did not make a sound, and her face barely changed.

"Are you okay?" I asked. I already knew she was in pain.

She merely nodded and held fast to that stoic façade of calm.

"You seem to be doing very well." Said a nurse as she peered from the monitor that registered contractions that seemed to belie my daughter's calm demeanor.

Again, she nodded.

A few minutes later, another one ripped through her. I looked at the monitor and knew it was a hard one. My daughter held her stance to the best of her ability.

However, this time, I watched as a small tear trailed down the side of her light caramel-colored face. She did not make a sound. Once again, she held her face expressionless and her body stiff. Only that tear let me know just how much pain she was in.

I leaned close to her ear and whispered, "I know you want to be strong for your baby and the world. But if you don't make a sound or move or let these people know that you are in pain, they will think you can do this all by yourself without any medication. Is that what you want?"

She did not answer me. However, when the next one hit, she simply said, "That really hurts."

Now, she did not yell it like I did when I was in the throes of a painful delivery. She said it just loud enough for the medical team to hear, and it was still only just above a whisper, "This hurts."

Then, the birthing team snapped into action and began to take measures to ensure my daughter would be more comfortable during this birthing process.

Yes. She was happy to see her baby come into the world.

She was happy that she had done her best not to act as if it were a painful experience. She never said, but I think she may have wanted to be able to tell her daughter that she braved her birth and was exceedingly happy that her daughter was here.

Not even her stoic child-birthing stance could hold up when the beautiful brown baby was placed in her arms. Even though the sleepiness of childbirth began to wash over her, she burst into a full, teeth-showing smile.

Though the moment with my granddaughter had passed, and as the country music began to seep back into my consciousness, I smiled broadly to myself because there was no doubt that my daughter was really happy when her daughter was born!

To know

If I knew then what I know now, I would have treasured times gone by.

I, like most folk, took so many things for granted. For example, by my birthday (November 27th), the weather would be cool enough for a jacket or coat. (I looked up the weather for my early childhood years, and it confirmed my memories.) The leaves began to turn shades of Fall in late September or early October. Grandmom made ice cream from the first snow, and she made preserves from the plums gathered from the tree in our backyard.

I should have treasured the times when we had four distinct seasons more, because today, global warming has everything topsy turvy, and some predict that we will come to a point where all the seasons will meld into one gigantic ball of fire. This is significant to me because I don't like the heat of summer. I love the beautiful colors of the flowers that bloom, and when the sky is blue, it is really blue. The daylight lasts longer, and butterflies are pretty cool. But the heat!

Okay, I have a better example!

I was a very active little girl, even before I started attending school. I played kickball, dodgeball, football, and baseball in our neighborhood. I swam and went to summer camp. I jumped single rope and double Dutch, and my hips twirled that hula hoop. I walked everywhere.

I never had a tricycle, and learning to ride without training wheels took me forever. I danced and danced and danced – ballet, toe, tap, modern jazz. Leaping and pirouetting. I tried basketball, and I was awful.

I ran track in junior high school but didn't like running all across the city for road work. I tried again in college because I wanted the uniform and name-brand running shoes they gave me. But they wanted me to run the 400 or 800-meter relays and I wanted to run the 50 or 100-yard dashes. They said my legs looked like a distance runners' legs.

They said I would get a second wind if I just kept going. I said my legs are dancers' legs, and I never get that second breath.

Then there was cheerleading. In high school, I tried, but they didn't choose me. I went ahead and tried again in college, and I made the squad. So, to all the other activities I enjoyed, I added splits in the air and jump splits that went from the air down to the floor in one fell swoop. A red and white skirt and sweater with matching Oxford shoes was our cheering oufit. The skirt was short, so we had little red briefs under it to protect our modesty. The skirt swayed as we walked. And it was something to behold when we stomped left, hit the right heel in the back, stomped left and stomped right, and repeated the sequence with the right foot stomping first. Our voices rang out in unison as we stomped and chanted through many cheers.

One time in college, we rode our bikes 15 miles one way, had a picnic, played volleyball and other running-around games, and then biked back those 15 miles. Man, I was sore the next day. As we peddled our day away in sheer happiness, feeling the wind in our faces was amazing.

Cheerleader red and white; ballet pink and white, black tap shoes, white and pink tights; blue bike; Nike tennis shoes in every color and stripe; African dance costumes; white or brown roller skates. Different costumes for different activities.

Skinned knees, busted lips, bruised skin, broken toe, stitches on my lip under my nose achieved during a racquetball game, twisted ankles on a miscued toe-dance. Nothing could stop the activity for long. Only a doctor told me to stop riding my bike, because I felt pain in my stomach after riding too far on my bicycle. I knew I had to listen only because I was told I was pregnant.

My point for writing about this is that in addition to all the time, all the activities, I also enjoyed the activity of eating. Butter Brickle ice cream is scrumptious on a walk from the bottom of Branch Avenue at Pennsylvania Avenue to the top of Branch and Alabama in Southeast

Washington, D.C. It would be so hot on that walk, and I would be about finished with that pint of ice cream by the time I reached the top. You could get a pint of ice cream for less than $100. What a treat, and I didn't gain a pound. I loved eating an entire 8-slice pizza (once I acquired a taste for pizza). I could down two hotdogs, a plate full of pork and beans, French fries, and a huge cup of Kool-Aid. Let's see, a honey bun with barbeque Fritos and a Pepsi was a delicious snack on the bus ride home from high school. A huge plate of nothing but candied sweet potatoes. Milk and Sugar Crisps cereal. An apple pie. Recess cups any time, any day, any amount!

Now I could eat like that because I never sat still. I was always on the move. I did not equate the ability to binge continuously with the ability to be active.

So, I kept my weight down and didn't worry about it. Well, life changed, and the next thing I knew, I was raising children, living life. I did not have much time for exercise or balancing eating with the level of exercise. And I looked up, and that proverbial nature took its course. Body parts expanded, and stuff just fell.

I still love to eat, but I now have to take more time to exercise. Yes, perhaps some of the more arduous moves I can only visualize in my mind because I can no longer jump as high or scissor split or complete four pirouettes or run too many lengths of that racquetball court.

But I see the moves, and I can instruct younger bodies in the mechanics of the moves. I still love it all. Yes, I have to cut back on my favorite foods. And because my body has become accustomed to extensive exercise and activity, I now have to work out almost as if I were in my twenties to keep things from getting too out of control.

Okay, that said, here is the real deal. The most important thing to admit is that if I knew then what I know now, *I would have been insufferable.*

Imagine my friends being invited over to my place for fun, only to discover that they will be served broccoli pops because ice cream will make you gain weight. Or, they thought they were going to play Barbie dolls, and I began to tell them about the anatomy of the girl doll as it relates to the relativity of the way the world spins around the sun. Or if they shared a story, and all I could add is that's a dangling participle, and perhaps we should hold our stomachs in while we share. I would have been so much fun to be around – wouldn't I?

If I had known then what I know now, what would I have done differently? Not a thing.

Just Do It: Leave My Grandson Alone!!

My mind wanders as I try to pay attention to those sharing their memoirs in my creative writing class. It works as long as they are sharing. But when a split second of quiet arises, my thoughts stray. Wow, this is on my heart. It's on my soul. Silence is golden. Keep things to yourself. Well, I cannot be silent. So, I'm just going to do it anyway.

The Godfather (Al Pacino) says something like, "Every time I try to get out, they pull me back in." It's wearying that the same theme keeps resurfacing time and time again. Why can't we, the people, get it together? My spirit is a little torn and aggravated. Why would a child on a school bus try to make another child perform oral sex on him, all the while calling him the "N" word? Why would the bus driver do nothing? Why weren't the police called? This is what happened to one of my grandsons yesterday. Nothing was to be done until this morning, when my daughter and son-in-law took my grandson to school. How could this happen in elementary school?!

I'm still distracted, and I am still having a little trouble concentrating on the wonderful memories that my creative writing classmates are sharing. I feel like I've been pulled back in time on two different fronts.

First, why can't whites move to a place where they understand that being Negro, Black, African American, non-white does not give them license to abuse or mistreat. At times, even I can be naïve enough to think that by now, my grandchildren would not have to hear these racial slurs flung at them.

To make it worse, you have some kid thinking he has the right to force my grandson into a sexual act, emboldened by the difference in color. The bus driver's inaction suggests he believes it is acceptable to overlook the urgency.

So far away; there are 3000 miles between the east and west coasts! I am limited in my ability to engage in physical touch, such as reaching out and holding my family. I have been impeded by a false or misplaced belief in the notion of the United States being the "land of the free." It's times like these that I pray. I'm not only praying for my daughter to do well in the parent/school faculty meeting. I am also praying that the Holy Spirit will massage my heart so that I will continue to have faith in mankind.

You may not know that at times like these, a person can easily be drawn into a place where they dislike all people who are not in their racial sphere. I know it is a test. So, I don't need to be reminded to hold on to God. I know we will get through this. I know about the high road. I know that I should not allow the actions and deeds of others to cause me to become what I hate.

I live the reality that time and distance can elicit even more intense emotions, because you cannot reach out and touch...

As I returned my attention to my class, I noticed that one of my creative writing classmates looked amazingly happy as she held her grandchild. Another classmate spoke about attending school with her grandson for such a joyous event.

Meanwhile, my family waits to hear what the school officials will say. I sit here three thousand miles away and wait for a phone call that will disclose their rationale and a solution.

Don't hate! God is love! I internally scream.

Have Hope! But I am tired and angry and frustrated and hurt. I felt all of these emotions when sexual assault happened to me!! I felt them even stronger when it happened to my daughter!!! And it could break me now that this happened to my grandchild!!!

I know that God is my strength, and my faith will be tested. Even with this knowledge, my faith grows stronger every day. This is one of those growth moments. This is one of those times when I cannot be pulled into the madness. So, if you pray, please pray for me.

All I have left to say... all I have left to demand is JUST DO IT ANYWAY – LEAVE MY GRANDSON ALONE!!!

The Art of the Smile

Ponderings of Rev. Dr. Elizabeth L.E. Wiggins

I love the arts. I thought to myself, "Yes, an easy topic."

I can write forever about the many ways I have been involved in the arts. Since I was a very young child, I've danced, sung, played violin, attempted to play piano, drawn, worked with stained glass, acted, written, directed, and worked with stage lighting and video. Several times, I have had the privilege of acting and being published. As a member of the audience, I have been amazed and cheered loudly at stage performances. Most of my life has been deeply entrenched in one art form or another. And I loved every minute of it.

I cannot help but smile as I think about how nature is full of artistic arrangements...

The sky is full of clouds that form different patterns every day. What a kaleidoscope of opportunity for the photographer or painter, of which I am neither.

The flowers that turn winter-dried gardens into kaleidoscopes of color do not bloom the same way each year.

One day, rain pounds down in torrents on my body, and the next, it lightly brushes my skin.

The sky, the flowers, the rain, all are works of art that only God can create. This makes me wonder whether we are all meant to be artists of one sort or another. I will have to hold on to that thought for a moment...

One day, I was driving across the 11th Street bridge in Southeast Washington, D.C., on my way to work. It was a sunny day, not a cloud in the sky. I looked out the front window. I had never seen such a beautiful rainbow. It was arching across the sky. That rainbow's colors were just as vivid as the one drawn on Lucky Charms cereal boxes. But this one was real. It was far enough in the distance that I could see it for quite a way across the bridge. I marveled at how beautifully clear it was. The rainbow seemed to have all the colors in the spectrum. It was faint at each edge, but the colors grew more vivid as the arch traveled toward the center from each side. Red, yellow, orange, green, blue... It was amazing.

More than 15 years later, I can see that rainbow as if I were seeing it painted on the sky this morning.

When you see a piece of art, it stays with you for a long time. Likewise, when you hear a work of art, you remember it for a long time.

Recently, I attended a National Symphony Orchestra concert. There I sat in the Kennedy Center after hearing the first part of the concert, completely unaware that what was to come would be breathtaking. More than 50 stringed instruments were on the stage, and the sound was amazing. The songs from Tchaikovsky's Romeo and Juliet filled that room, and I thought, wow, this sounds like a taped recording. The pure sound moved me, and I found myself thinking of things from my childhood, and my mind began to wander...

I played in my elementary school orchestra. I was a "budding" violinist. I was good enough to play for graduation. We always wore blue or black skirts with white shirts.

We would line up, march in, and take our seats. Violins and bows ready, we would strike our notes. Hum hum hum hum hum (humming "Pomp and Circumstance). Our parents were probably amazed that we actually made music. I had come a long way from the screeching sounds my bow and violin would create early in my training. Today, I wonder why my parents never told me to cut out that noise. Now, that is a sign of loving parents. Reflecting on my childlike efforts to create art brings a smile to my face.

By the time I was in junior high school, I played well enough to sit in the second chair in the orchestra. There was another girl in my class who could really play. She even knew how play using the vibrato technique. Vibrato is where the violinist shakes his/her fingers back and forth on the strings while running the bow across the strings. It creates a wavering sound. She made it look so easy. I could not and still cannot do it.

Anyway, we would play this train song. The sound our strings created actually sounded like a train. I can hear the accent on the first beat of each four-beat measure. Vroom, vroom, vroom, vroom. Vroom, vroom, vroom, vroom. First beat long, next beat short. We played on and on, doing our part to play the background to the melody that played above it. All the bows were going in the same direction. It was complete precision for such young instrumentalists. The sound still rings melodiously in my mind even today...

About seven years ago, I decided to take up the violin again. I took lessons and was surprised that I could play pretty well.

But then, four years ago, my grandson decided he wanted to play. So, I put my *budding* come back on hold, and let him use my violin because many public schools no longer had instruments on hand for the students to use. What a shame.

I went to his first recital, and it was pretty good. His 8th grade concert went very well. All the students played well. I, the proud grandmom, recorded him playing. Afterward, I took pictures of him holding his violin, and other pictures captured him with his siblings and mother celebrating his accomplishment. Looks like he may continue where I left off. Maybe he'll play in college. I'm glad the beautiful love of instrumental music lives on...

A smile came to my face as I thought about the first time I played, and then hearing my grandson play. What a treasure!

I was lost in the musical tones of the National Symphony Orchestra. The beauty of that art mingles with my memories and remains with me like the splendor of that rainbow...

Then I began to wonder whether there was an art to my smile. Is it artistic amazement that leads to such a bright smile? Can't we all exude the art of creating a world where we smile, and kindness radiates from our core?

I sometimes wonder why so many seniors no longer smile very much.

I find myself smiling countless times during the day.

Is smiling an art form?

I am a senior. The essence of the smile is important to me. I watch my fellow senior citizens and note that we are not always as kind as we should be. Maybe that is because we have seen so much and endured so much. Maybe we have hoped, and our hopes have not been realized. So, maybe we just stopped hoping. I will not judge their reasons. I would like to encourage their smile. Perhaps a couple of examples that I have witnessed would help.

I was coming out of the dressing stall at a swimming pool after an aqua-fit class. I heard a voice with no hint of kindness, "You are not allowed to hold up a stall while you take a shower."

"I didn't take a shower," I began.

With a wrinkled brow and without a smile in sight, she replied, "I don't care. It doesn't matter. You are not supposed to do it."

"I needed to use the bathroom. I could not hold it, so I went to the bathroom." I returned to the stall and continued to get dressed. I wonder why she accused me instead of asking.

Anyway, I usually get into the pool about 3 minutes late. Partly because the traffic going past two schools on the way is always hectic. When I got into the pool, I quickly learned that the ladies have spots in the pool. They seem to have a problem if you take their space. Whenever they arrive, that spot is still theirs – no excuse me, they just come to stand right up on you. It's the oddest thing. So, I just ease over to the side and wait until everyone has their space, and then I take whatever space is left.

As I walk to class, I say, "Good morning." I get a frown or a mean stare in response. Perhaps we believe we are putting forth an air of maturity.

However, it comes off as being just plain mean.

Why don't we smile more? Is it a burden that we have lived for more than half a century? Is it a badge of honor to reach senior citizen status and then refuse to smile? Whatever the thinking, why aren't we happy? What can we do to help each other exude happiness occasionally?

I'm not saying that we need to take a stand and be strong and hearty.

I'm talking about the everyday way in which we live. I'm talking about the way others perceive us. Sometimes, I hesitate to speak because the look I get says don't you dare!

I have been through many trials and hardships. But I seem to be more and more grateful for each day. And I really only want to be as kind as I can.

It's artistic. Everyone gifted and talented in some form of artistic expression should practice it.

They should be conscious of doing well. They should hone their art and want the world to know they are good at it. Why not think of being an intentionally smiling senior as an art form? And, like most art forms, I believe it is in danger of becoming extinct.

We have to return to a place where we seek reasons to smile.

What do all the other artistic abilities mean – if our seniors have lost their reason to smile?

What use is it to sing melodically if our seniors find no joy they can take from it; if it does not ignite a spark or elicit a lingering smile, then is the effort in vain?

I don't know, but I pray that my desire to smile never dims as I grow older. The idea that our seniors have lost their smiles makes me sad. Thank goodness it doesn't cause me to lose my smile. I hope I will continue to see that rainbow and hear the melodious tones of the violin; I will always marvel at the shapes of clouds and different patterns that are formed by the rain.

Not only do I want to remember, but I pray that I create new reasons to smile and new opportunities to make others smile. I never want to lose the art of my inner and outer smile.

P.S. Seems like my prayers were heard. Today Is Friday, May 5, 2023, and at the pool today, folks were smiling and saying good morning. The atmosphere was charged with happy energy that just caused my smile to grow brighter.

I wonder if I touch my nose with my tongue, would that make you smile? Let's see.

Oh, I saw you smile!

A Short Thought About Mail

Mail. You might ask if folk still use the mail. Definitely they do, even though, for most, it is not an everyday occurrence. I usually mail cards at Christmas. But about ten years ago, my church began having a Christmas mailbox where members could drop off their Christmas cards. The wonderful team of volunteer Christmas mail sorters would give the cards to the addressees. This service was offered on each of the four Advent Sundays leading up to Christmas Day. That seasonal activity allowed more members to share cards without worrying about the expense of purchasing stamps. I had even gotten in the habit of making about ten cards and addressing them to visitors. That way, visitors could also receive a Christmas greeting.

I still sent cards out in the mail to friends who were not members of the church. Not only that, it is always nice to send cards to others throughout the year. I send cards to let people know I'm thinking about them. So, mail continues to be a useful means of correspondence for me.

However, I found a new appreciation for the mail system this past Christmas. I hadn't attended church for a minute, but I still wanted to send Christmas greetings to my church family. I went to the post office and bought 150 stamps. I then went to the Hallmark Store and bought all sorts of Christmas Cards. They all had generic messages. So, I still went home and created a message that told of my love of the Christmas season.

I addressed envelopes, put on the stamps, and took them to the post office, and I was happy because Christmas greetings were on their way through the mail. I was really getting into that Christmas spirit. Tree up! Cards out! Don't have to cook this year because plans were already set to go out.

All I had to do was sit back and enjoy the season.

Now, this was just after things were beginning to return to normal following COVID-19. The mail had slacked and stalled, and sometimes, we would not receive our mail until extremely late in the day. So, I wasn't expecting anything at all during the season.

But then it started. For about three weeks, cards began coming in each day. You wouldn't think that getting a Christmas card would mean so much. I had received them before. But there was something about this year that made it mean the world to me. Maybe it was because I hadn't been attending service. Or maybe it was just the spirit of Christmas shining through. But each card made me happy.

I usually will quickly look at the outside of the card and then check who it is from. I will hang it on a wall in my living room so visitors can view it when they stop by. But the emotion overtook me this year, and I found myself reading each card and smiling.

Yes, it was probably because I was not on good terms with the church experience, and I really missed my church friends. Not worshipping God with them in that building was a spiritual loss. I sent the cards as usual, but I usually only expect to receive a few. This year I received 75 cards. And only two people sent the same card. Imagine my surprise!!

I also received phone calls from people who had not sent cards. It was such a profound and spirit-filled moment, and I am still deeply moved. I did not hang the cards on the walls this year. Instead, I placed each card under my Christmas tree. Each card had a special place. I don't want to downplay my appreciation for the gifts. However, for some reason, I thought these cards were valuable gifts.

ABOUT THREE WEEKS AGO, I was again surprised to get a letter in the mail.

My dear friend from college had sent me a letter. We both live in Maryland, but we do not get to see each other very often. We send each other birthday cards and Christmas cards.

But this time, it was a letter. A handwritten letter sharing what was going on in her life and updating me on the news from our alma mater. I could not stop smiling. A handwritten letter. Can you imagine that in this day and time? I thought I had been filled with joy after receiving the Christmas cards, but this was just as wonderful. Life's simple pleasures. I know we can text, and I know we can email. But, man! It is nice to get a handwritten letter.

So, you know I had to write her back. Okay, my handwriting is horrible. So, I typed a letter, created a nice letterhead, and sent it to her. As a result of our exchanging these letters, we have made time to have lunch today.

I am excited and looking forward to it.

MAIL. SENDING LETTERS, notes and cards helps strengthen relationships. Mail is not obsolete. And besides, it is just a nice thing to do for the sender and the receiver. So, never give up on the mail.

Thank God for Guidance?

I watched a young lady give the offertory appeal and prayer during a worship service. Her white skirt was extremely short. I have a feeling she felt good about how she looked when she left home. However, as she spoke from the pulpit, she continuously tried to pull the skirt down. I surmised that she began to feel self-conscious.

My heart went out to her. She has so many learning experiences ahead of her. She will be tested so many times as she grows and matures. Maybe she truly believed that the skirt would be appropriate for worship service. But God has a way of working on you, and we mere older mortals hope she can hear and will listen, better than we sometimes did when we were her age.

I pray no one will say anything unsettling to her. Perhaps instead they can allow the Holy Spirit to continue the work that began at that moment. Those of us who have been there and had to decide whether to wear or not to wear an outfit may have listened sometimes and, other times, paid no heed. Whatever the case, we had to learn.

I am reminded of my Mom, grandmom, aunts, and other women who would direct and guide me even after I became an adult.

"That is too short." or "Now, Elizabeth, do you really think you should wear that?"

But they lived by example. My Mom never wore a skirt shorter than the tops of her calves or just below her knees. She always wore stockings. She did wear makeup but did not allow us to wear makeup. And only unpierced earrings hung from her ears. A photo of my Mom still sits on the piano in the home where we grew up. She was a woman known for not liking to take photos. However, in that photo, she was captured as a slim, trim, slightly smiling woman with dancing eyes wearing a stylish blouse and sporting an up-to-date hairstyle. In her younger years, my Mom would have been what they would have called a fox. She loved to dance and have a good time. She didn't drink much.

By the way, my Dad was the same. Dressed well and appropriate for any occasion. At a picnic, he wore picnic clothes. At church, he wore a suit. At work, he wore a suit. At social gatherings, he dressed appropriately. My grandparents were the same.

I don't have to imagine what they were like in their older adult years because I was right there with them. Such a blessing they all were. My maternal grandparents watched us while our parents were working.

I have visions of my Mom and Dad doing the stroll, a dance they did in the 50s. They would stroll dressed to the nines wearing fancy and stylish clothes. Sparkle covered dresses and dapper suits were worn to the club, but A-line skirts and crisp white blouses for church. Men wore suits and the hats were removed as they came indoors

My Mom would tell us how she would be scolded when she got in my grandmother's way.

I can see my Mom questioning my grandmom about something happening in the house where she worked. "Mom, why are they doing that?"

"Don't you mess up with my white folk," would be my grandmother's response.

I always remember my grandmother as Grandmom. I never remember seeing her dance. I remember seeing her usher at church and put on church plays. She combed my hair, and I combed her hair. I remember sitting with her while we crocheted or knitted together.

One day recently, I went to my closet and pulled out a dress I usually liked to wear.

As I was holding the dress, I heard a voice say, "Now, are you really going to wear that." I shuddered and shook my head as I carefully returned the frock to the closet. I knew the time had passed for me to wear that garb.

I pondered these things during that worship service. I am not sure why I went down this road thinking about these memories. Sometimes, I allow my mind to go where it will and see what materializes. Perhaps I was thinking about that scripture that says, "Train up a child in the way they should go, and they will not stray far from it." (Proverbs 22:6)

I know I will continue to advise and gently guide my children and grandchildren just as my parents and grandparents did for me. Perhaps they will listen, and perhaps they won't. Lord knows I did not always listen.

As I watched that young lady tug at the hem of her skirt, I know that, too, I have been in the "pulling my skirt down" situation. I am grateful for the guidance I received. Moving forward, I pray that the Holy Spirit will prick her. It's priceless when we find ourselves a little off center during those crucial decision-making processes.

Thank God for Guidance – I know I still need it.

Am I My Hair?

I am chuckling today as I push these braids out of my face to join those that are going back down my back.

No, this is not my natural hair, and I have no problem letting you know it is not mine. The braids are a convenience. We have many conveniences—hair, microwaves, spanks, technology, and colored contact lenses.

So, let me say to you, the reader or hearer, "Be careful! Or, you might wake up one day and realize you made a great big mistake!!"

I remember a sermon I did a few years ago. I spoke about the fallacy of attributing our worth to external features and characteristics. To make my point, I used the words of India Arie – "I am not my hair." I preached about how I shouldn't be judged by my hair.

To be real, one day, my hair may be long. Another day, it may be short. One day, it may be curly; one day, it may be straight. One day, braided; another day, I will be sporting extensions. "I am not my hair!" I would exclaim.

My confidence was high because I knew that I could change my hairstyle. I felt sure and ardent about my crusade to encourage listeners to lighten up on the ridiculing witticism directed at women about their hair.

I said all this because at that time I had a decent length of hair. I could style or not style my hair. An afro was manageable. Curls could be in a bob, snatchback, or the latest shortcut. My smile would brighten as I patted my hair following a trip to the hairdresser that ended with me having a new hairdo.

Even on a bad hair day, I was okay because I knew I was just being lazy and could fix the mess that stared back at me from the mirror. It is easy to offer care and concern for others when you think this situation does not apply to you....

Then, one day in my mid-fifties, that all changed. I was taking some medicine that didn't agree with my body chemistry, which allowed my hair to grow. My hair began to come out in clumps. The next thing I knew, my hair was no longer than one of my stumpy fingernails. I could do nothing with it.

The lack of hair and the shape of my bald head caused me to rethink things. Maybe I was my hair!

Unlike many women with short hair, mine had no natural curl or wave. It was kinky and unruly. Random strands of hair would poke up without any rhyme or reason, or permission from the owner of the head. It wasn't easy to comb. The products made for my hair did nothing. I could not encourage it to grow or behave.

I then began to remember the days when I would gel the hair on the sides of my head. This process was supposed to make my hair lie down and look like I was sporting a short haircut. Well, no more!

Now, I still had to go to work. You did not get a pass because you believed your hair looked crazy. There was no long-term disability relief for unruly hair or self-imposed culture shock. So, I had to go to work. As my hair came out, my vanity grew stronger. I could not go to work looking like this.

It was amazing how folks in the office suddenly did not recognize me. They would walk past me and do a double-take, sometimes a triple-take, before they realized I was the person they had worked with for years.

I became so self-conscious that I began wearing headwraps, headbands, and hats to work. Anything to cover my head so I could have a tiny measure of peace of mind. No one said a word to me. They may have gawked, wondering why I wore those headdresses, but they did not say anything. Slowly but surely, over two years, I began to feel the insecurity I felt as a child.

Nevertheless, my hair would not and did not grow. I could not get a weave or extensions because there was nothing to attach them to. I could not wear a wig because it made me too hot. Hot flashes and wigs do not go together!

Then I woke up one morning, and my mental light went off. "Boy, when you make mistakes, you really make whoppers, don't you?" I chastised myself as I realized the mistake I had made. I was just about to don my daily headwrap. By the way, it had to match my outfit to a tee. I stopped mid-wrap and looked at myself in the mirror. I put the wrap down, placed my hands on the sink, and stared ahead. "Why are you tying up your head? Because there isn't really any hair to cover. And it is still you under that wrap. Besides, I thought you were not your hair!!"

At that moment, I decided to go to work and show my hair. Dressed and prepped with my hair out, off I went to work.

People asked what happened. Others offered me hair-growing solutions. After a while, I turned them down and told them I was fine with the length of my hair. It is what it is. If my hair is not going to grow anymore, then I will just be grateful for the length it is.

I would not wear any more headwraps. I would no longer waste money buying hair treatments. I will become comfortable in my skin. I will practice what I preach. So, my prayers changed, and I gave thanks. Cliché? Yep.

But I did pray.

And as a result of prayer – that's just what I did. I became comfortable with my short hair. I brushed it down. Some days, I would slick it down to my head. On other days, I let it do what it wanted.

I don't know when my hair began to grow again. However, I looked up one day and I was sporting a short Afro.

Some days, I would add hair products that naturally curled it. On other days, I would just pick it out and wear my natural hair. And there are still plenty of days where I would just let it do what it wanted to do.

Within another year, it was long enough to braid and curl.

I swim now, so it is more convenient to wear it braided. Now I have extensions, but my hair is long enough to style.

Not everyone believes in the power of God, the power of prayer. But I genuinely believe I am better equipped to minister because I now have another example of what it feels like to go without a part of me that I took for granted.

Honestly, I have never had hair that went way down my back. But I was used to having hair that would grow. Even when I cut it, it would grow back.

I woke up and realized I had made the mistake of permitting vanity to make me lose sight of the call to be humble and grateful.

Lesson learned: If you have long hair, be grateful. If you have short hair, be grateful. If you are bald, be thankful. After all, it is a big mistake to think for a moment that you are your hair!!

Something Treasured: My Grandfather Clock

Okay, just in case they read this piece, let me get this out of the way so there is no confusion. Above and beyond everything else, my treasures are the relationships I have with my husband, my children, and my grandchildren. Better known as Langford, Jr., Lauren, Lynne, Langford, III, Carliece, Kevonte, Kalvin, Logan, Leora, Luke, Kyrie, and Lex.

I am beginning to recognize that material things just don't seem to mean the same. It is not the material value of the thing that matters. It is rather the nurturing of my familial relationships that occurs as a result of having those things.

That said, I tried to think of an object that can illustrate my treasured love of relationships.

As I was thinking about writing a memoir about treasures, I became really excited. I began to realize why I hold on to some things (like greeting cards).

I really do get extremely excited when the proverbial light bulb goes off. Times when I can connect the dots. This writing experience has definitely helped me connect some dots.

Let me ponder treasure. I could write about the crocheted tablecloth my Mom made and gave me as a wedding gift. It's more than 36 years old, and I still pull it out on special occasions. I thought about the orange, yellow, and white blanket I crocheted when I was in my late teens. I took it to college to use on my dorm room bed. My granddaughter now covers up with that crocheted blanket. All are treasures for sure.

Nevertheless, I think I will write about a grandfather's clock. Yep, a grandfather's clock.

Imagine three boys, three girls, a mother, and a father doing chores in a small three-story semi-detached brick house. The call came bright and early on Saturday mornings. We had to do chores before we could go to scouting, dancing, to the movies, or hang out with friends.

"Come on, you all get up!" That was my Mom's voice.

"Did you hear your mother? Get moving!" That was Dad reinforcing Mom's call. It was meant to encourage their tired, stretching, and blinking kids to get the sleep out of their bones and start the day.

"Elizabeth, did you get the dust rags and the pledge?" Mom asked.

"Yep, got it," I said to her as I held up that yellow can of furniture polish.

Maybe it is a small house. But it still seemed like everything in our home as made from wood. There were hardwood floors, a wooden China closet, a buffet, a table and chairs, a coffee table and end tables, a television and hi-fi, and a piano and woodwork. Wood, wood, wood! Everything was made of wood, and my sisters and I would have to polish each piece to a glossy sheen.

Come on, boys, let's get the mops and Mr. Clean. Pull out the Johnson's paste wax and the buffer so we can get moving on the floors." My Dad got my brothers started on the chores.

Of course, if it was a sunny day, we had to be diligent.

"Hold up," my mom would call out. "Look at those windows." The sunshine was not our friend because it was showing all of the whitish/pinkish streaks left behind from our cleaning. We thought we had done a good job with that newspaper. But at her cautioning words, we turned around and went back to the task.

I think my parents knew something about how to get us energized because the music seemed to put a pep in our step. We would be up mopping floors, dusting all those wooden surfaces, wiping down walls and floorboards, and cleaning the kitchen appliances.

We had an old-fashioned hi-fi. You know, the one that was made of wood and was long. It had a turntable, speaker, and radio built into a piece of furniture.

All eight of us would be moving around the house, and you could hear us singing at the tops of our lungs. We were all blessed with good singing voices. We would be cleaning, singing, and dancing.

One song my Mom loved to sing was the 'Grandfather's Clock , written by Henry Clay Work in 1876. I chuckle out loud and sway, just remembering the words to that song.

My grandfather's clock
It was too large for the shelf
So it stood ninety years on the floor" It was taller by half
Than the old man himself
Though it weighed not a pennyweight more It was bought on the morn
Of the day that he was born
And was always his treasure and pride But it stopped short
But it stopped short. Never to go again When the old man died
Rags swished across the table and chairs as my sisters and I nodded to the beat.
Ninety years without slumbering Tick, tock, tick, tock
My brothers' floor-scrubbing movements seemed to be in complete sync with the rhythm of the tune.
His life seconds numbering Tick, tock, tick, tock
It stopped short Never to go again
All eight of us would stop on a dime, holding our positions until the last words of the refrain were done.
When the old man died

Then we picked up the rhythm of the dancing, singing, and cleaning, only pausing when we had sung the song so many times that we all knew it was time for a new song.

Well, I think my Mom loved that song because she always wanted a grandfather clock and never was able to get one. I guess she passed that love of grandfather clocks down to me. Her dream became my dream. I held onto her dream and eventually bought a grandfather clock. Just like the one in the song, it is too tall to sit on a shelf.

So, it sits on the floor in the corner of the room. It's about 7 feet tall and made of a sort of cherry-colored wood. It has several melodies that can be set to chime. It ticks and tocks the seconds away. It chimes on the quarter, half, and hour, reminding us that it's never too late until it stops. You can watch the movement too.

Perhaps the chiming of the clock is annoying to some. But I love it. There are times when I sit and watch the movement of the clock's hands, remembering happy times. And while it reminds me of times long ago, it also brings hope for what is to come.

I hope that when my children read this or hear me talking about the ties that bind us, they will want to hold onto that grandfather clock. Again, not so much for the monetary value that may come from the fact that there is a brass plate that deems it an heirloom. Rather, because the grandfather clock ties our generations together through my Mom's dream.

It's a catchy tune that reminds us to treasure the time we have with our loved ones. Back in the 1960s and 70s, it was just our family of eight bopping and cleaning, passing the time, doing chores, and having family time. It was a time when my young mind thought my parents would live forever. The clock might stop. The man might die, but my parents seemed ageless.

Today, it is a reminder that my mother had a dream that I shared. I was able to purchase a grandfather clock and share it with her before she died. And, that yes, indeed, one life does end at the stop of the tick-tocking of their internal clock.

But our lives continue, and the generations increase. Yes, by itself, my grandfather clock is merely a piece of furniture. However, that same grandfather clock combined with that song is a treasured memory that binds generations. It can bind the past, present, and future generations because my Mom sang a song and had a dream.

Time with my grandfather clock is something treasured indeed.

Did you love *Living While Liz*? Then you should read *Living While Liz*[1] by ELIZABETH WIGGINS!

Living While Liz

Vivre pendant que Liz

By Elizabeth Wiggins

[2]

This memoir takes the reader on a fun, educational, spirit-filled cantor through episodes in the life of Rev. Dr. Elizabeth Lynne Ellis Wiggins. Despite the introductory titles, this book is not a lofty, hard-to-understand piece of literature. The author wants the reader to discover self in some of her experiences. She wants you to laugh out loud, shed a tear, nod your head, and just plain old enjoy yourself. This book is for everyone! The topics are written in a creative way intended to cause the reader to enjoy thinking. As you begin a chapter, you will find yourself wanting to finish it and quickly move to the next one. The author hopes you will find something to share with someone else. This book is being released in English with a French translation as well.

---

1. https://books2read.com/u/bW8kvz

2. https://books2read.com/u/bW8kvz

Please note that the author is neither a professional writer in either English nor natively fluent in French. Nevertheless, you will come to understand why she decided to release the book in both languages. The chapter titles are meant to entice you to read further and discover what could possibly be in store for you. Imagine the possibilities of reading about shoe laces, being green, long-termers, and a clock. You just may not stop with one read. Perhaps you will read it again and share it in a book club or discussion group. If you are an educator perhaps you will read and teach it in English and in French! Working in ministry, you, too, may find this book useful. Come along and join the author by reading the cleverly written antics of Living While Liz!!

www.ingramcontent.com/pod-product-compliance
Lightning Source LLC
Chambersburg PA
CBHW031846090426
42741CB00005B/372